R-2947-NIC

Racial Disparities in the Criminal Justice System

Joan Petersilia

June 1983

Prepared for
The National Institute of Corrections,
U.S. Department of Justice

SANTA MONICA, CA. 90406

PREFACE

Over the last three decades, social science researchers have repeatedly addressed the possibility of racial discrimination in the criminal justice system, but it remains an open question. Because of problems with data and methodology, no study has established definitively that the system does or does not discriminate against racial minorities.

This two-year study approached the issue by comparing the treatment of white and minority offenders at key decision points in the system, from arrest through release from custody, and by investigating possible racial differences in criminal behavior that might influence that treatment. It attempted to overcome the material and methodological limitations of earlier research in two ways:

- By using both official records and information from a large sample of prison inmates about aspects of their background and criminal behavior, and
- By using multiple regression techniques when possible to analyze the resulting data, techniques that allow the analyst to control for other factors besides race that might affect the system's handling of minority offenders.

The study was supported by the National Institute of Corrections, Bureau of Prisons, U.S. Department of Justice. The report should be of interest to criminal justice researchers who are investigating the system's operations, and to policymakers who are looking for mechanisms that will ensure equal treatment for offenders, regardless of race. Because the study deals with a complex and sensitive issue, the report describes the data, methodology, and findings in considerable, technical detail. To accommodate readers who are more concerned with policy than with research, the report includes a short Executive Summary of the study's conclusions and policy implications.

EXECUTIVE SUMMARY

I. INTRODUCTION AND SUMMARY

Critics of the criminal justice system view the arrest and imprisonment rates for blacks and other minorities as evidence of racial discrimination. Although the laws governing the system contain no racial bias, these critics claim that where the system allows discretion to criminal justice officials in handling offenders, discrimination can, and often does, enter in. They argue that blacks, for example, who make up 12 percent of the national population, could not possibly commit 48 percent of the crime—but that is exactly what their arrest and imprisonment rates imply. Defenders of the system argue that the statistics do not lie, and that the system does not discriminate but simply reacts to the prevalence of crime in the black community.

Statistics on street crime lend support to this argument. An astonishing 51 percent of black males living in large cities are arrested at least once for an index crime during their lives, compared with only 14 percent of white males.[1] Fully 18 percent of black males serve time, either as juveniles or adults, compared with 3 percent of white males (Greenfeld, 1981). Blacks are also disproportionately victimized by crime: Murder is the leading cause of death for young black males, and is also high for young black females.

Crime, then, is a fact of life in the ghetto. Blacks and other minorities must deal with crime and the criminal justice system much more than whites. Moreover, as crime rates continue to rise, the nation's overcrowded prisons find their economic and operational problems compounded by racial problems. In many prisons, racial gangs maneuver for dominance and victimize racial minorities—and whites are often a minority. These conditions have given rise to the question of racial discrimination; to address it, our study pursued three objectives:

(1) To discover whether there is any evidence that the criminal justice system systematically treats minorities differently from whites;

(2) If there is such evidence, to see whether that treatment represents discrimination or is simply a reaction to the amount of crime committed by minorities; and

---

[1]Blumstein and Graddy, 1981. Index offenses are murder, rape, robbery, assault, burglary, larceny/theft, auto theft, and arson.

(3) To discuss the policy implications for correcting any bias.

METHODOLOGY AND DATA

Social science researchers have been addressing the question of discrimination in the system for more than thirty years, but have failed to reach consensus on almost every point. Studies have offered evidence both for and against racial bias in arrest rates, prosecution, conviction, sentencing, corrections, and parole. There are many reasons for these contradictions. Some studies have data bases too small to permit any generalization. Others have failed to control for enough (or any) of the other factors that might account for apparent racial discrimination. Most studies have looked at only one or two levels of the system. And no studies have examined criminals' pre-arrest contact with the system—a point at which many believe the greatest racial differences in treatment exist.

We attempted to overcome those shortcomings by using data from official records and prisoner self-reports, by examining the evidence for discrimination throughout the criminal justice system, and by controlling for the major variables that might create the appearance of discrimination. Whenever the data were sufficient to do so, we used multiple regression analyses of system decisions and criminal behavior to control for the most obvious variables. In the comparisons, then, the offenders were somewhat "interchangeable" except for race.

The study data came from two sources: the California Offender-Based Transaction Statistics (OBTS) for 1980, and the Rand Inmate Survey (RIS). The OBTS is a computerized information system maintained by the California Bureau of Criminal Statistics that tracks the processing of offenders from arrest to sentencing. The RIS consists of data obtained from self-reports of approximately 1400 male prison inmates in California, Michigan, and Texas.

MAJOR FINDINGS

We found some racial differences in both criminal behavior and the treatment of offenders in the states involved. (See Table S.1.)

Racial Differences in Case Processing

Although the case processing system generally treated offenders similarly, we found racial differences at two key points: Minority sus-

Table S.1

Summary of Study Findings

Element Studied	Evidence of Racial Differences[a]
Offender Behavior	
Preference for different crime types	+
Volume of crime committed	0
Crime motivation	++
Type of weapon preferred and extent of its use	++
Victim injury	+
Need for drug and alcohol treatment	0
Need for vocational training and education	+
Assessments of prison program effects	0
Arrest	
Probability of suffering arrest	0
Whether arrested on warrant or probable cause*	+
Probability of having case forwarded to prosecutor*	+
Prosecution and Sentencing	
Whether case is officially filed*	+
Type of charges filed*	0
Reasons for nonprosecution*	+
Whether the case is settled by plea bargaining*	+
Probability of conviction*	0
Type of crime convicted of*	0
Type of sentence imposed*	++
Length of sentence imposed	+
Corrections	
Type of programs participated in	0
Reasons for not participating in programs	0
Probability of having a work assignment	0
Length of sentence served	++
Extent and type of prison infractions	++

SOURCES: The OBTS for starred (*) items; the RIS for all others.

[a]0 = none; + = suggestive trend; ++ = statistically significant.

pects were more likely than whites to be released after arrest; however, after a felony conviction, minority offenders were more likely than whites to be given longer sentences and to be put in prison instead of jail.

Racial Differences in Post-Sentencing Treatment

In considering participation in treatment and work programs and the reasons inmates gave for not participating, we found no statistically significant differences that implied discrimination against minorities in corrections. However, in looking at length of sentence served, we found significant racial differences in California and Texas, but none in Michigan. These findings held even when we controlled for other major factors that might affect release decisions. In California prisons, blacks and Hispanics serve longer sentences than whites—largely, however, because of racial differences in court-imposed sentences. In Texas, minorities also serve longer sentences— appreciably longer than their court-imposed minimum terms. In Michigan the reverse is true. There, blacks enter prison with longer sentences than whites, but serve roughly the same time.

Racial Similarities in Crime Commission Rates and Probability of Arrest

The high post-arrest release rates for minorities do not indicate that police overarrest minorities *in proportion to the kind and amount of crime they actually commit*. We found that annualized crime commission rates were much the same among white and minority criminals. Moreover, there are no consistent, statistically significant, racial differences in the probability of arrest, given that an offender has committed a crime.

Racial Differences in Offender Behavior

There are some evident racial differences in criminal motivation, weapons use, and prison behavior, but most are not statistically significant. Blacks rated economic distress higher than other motivations, but not significantly more so than other groups. Whites rated hedonistic motives for crime significantly higher than blacks or Hispanics. In weapons use, there were only two significant findings. Hispanics were much more likely than the other groups to use knives, and black burglars were less likely to be armed. Racial differences were strongest in prison behavior. In Texas, blacks had a higher rate of infractions; in California, whites did.

CONCLUSIONS

These findings raise some important questions and identify some patterns that, together with other research, suggest tentative conclusions.

Disparities in Release Rates

Because we found that minorities do not have a higher probability of arrest, the release rates might be explained by evidentiary problems. Prior research indicates that prosecutors do have greater problems making minority cases "stick" because victims often have difficulty identifying minority suspects. Moreover, minority victims and witnesses often refuse or fail to cooperate after an arrest is made. Some racial differences in release rates may also result from the fact that police more often arrest white suspects than minority suspects "on warrant." Since the evidentiary criteria for issuing warrants approximate those for filing charges, it seems reasonable that fewer whites than minorities would be released without charges.

Disparities in Sentencing and Time Served

Controlling for the other major factors that might influence sentencing and time served, we found that minorities receive harsher sentences and serve longer in prison—other things being equal. However, racial differences in plea bargaining and jury trials may explain some of the difference in length and type of sentence. Plea bargaining resolves a higher percentage of felony cases involving white defendants, whereas jury trials resolve a higher percentage of cases involving minorities. Although plea bargaining ensures conviction, it also virtually guarantees a reduced charge or a lighter sentence, or both; conviction by a jury usually results in more severe sentencing.

Differences in sentencing and time served may also reflect the kinds of information that judges and parole boards use to make their decisions. Research has found that in 80 percent of cases, judges follow the sentencing recommendation made in the probation officer's pre-sentence investigation report (PSR). Moreover, in many states, the PSR becomes the heart of the parole board's case-summary file. These reports are usually very comprehensive "portraits" of offenders, containing personal and socioeconomic information, as well as any details the probation officer can get on their criminal habits and attitudes. This information can be, and evidently is, assessed for indicators of recidivism—that is, traits related to the probability that a released offender will return to crime. Blacks and Hispanics may have more such traits than whites (e.g., past unemployment).

The relation between court-imposed sentence and length of time served supports these conjectures. Minorities *received* longer minimum sentences than whites in all three states. However, that sentence had varying effects on time finally *served*. In California, racial differences in sentence served corresponded roughly to the differences in court-imposed sentences. In Texas, time served was appreciably longer for minorities than for whites—and appreciably longer than the court-imposed sentence. In Michigan, the reverse was true: There, blacks received longer court-imposed sentences than whites, but served roughly the same time.

California has a determinate sentencing policy, which explains the relation of sentence imposed to sentence served there. But the contrast between Texas and Michigan can perhaps be explained by parole practices. Texas has a highly individualized process that incorporates the full range of an inmate's criminal history and personal and socioeconomic characteristics. In contrast, Michigan has adopted a risk-assessment formula for parole decisions that relies primarily on indicators of personal culpability such as juvenile record, violence of conviction crime, and prison behavior. This practice evidently avoids racial disparities in time served—and may overcome the racial disparity in court-imposed sentences.

Nevertheless, overcoming racial disparities in time served is not the definitive objective of parole boards. Their primary responsibility is to decide whether releasing an inmate will endanger society. By ignoring socioeconomic and other extralegal indicators of recidivism, they may reduce racial disparities in parole decisions, but they may do so at the expense of putting probable recidivists back on the street.

Indicators of Recidivism

If recidivism indicators are valid and explain racial disparities in sentencing and time served, the system is not discriminating. It is simply reflecting the larger racial problems of society, and it can do little about the overrepresentation of minorities in prison. However, the RIS data and some other research contain suggestions that the recidivism indicators may not be so "racially neutral" after all.

Minorities are overrepresented in the criminal population, relative to their proportion of the national population. However, they do constitute roughly half the criminal population. Thus, within that population, their characteristics should have no more effect on empirically derived indicators of recidivism than the characteristics of white recidivists—unless minorities have higher crime commission rates. We have found, however, that minorities and whites have similar crime commission rates, and other research has established that whites and minorities have approximately the same probability of recidivism. It is apparent that some indicators of recidivism overlap with race in ways that deserve investigation.

IMPLICATIONS FOR FUTURE RESEARCH AND POLICY

These findings and conclusions suggest some important research needs and policy initiatives. Among the research priorities are:

- Documenting the reasons for post-arrest/pre-filing release rates and controlling for race of the offender and type of arrest;
- Analyzing post-arrest problems with witnesses to discover whether and how the race of the suspect and/or of the witness affects cooperation;
- Determining the relation of plea bargaining and jury trials to race, and why minority defendants are less likely to plea-bargain;
- Establishing the reasons why minorities receive and serve longer sentences, paying particular attention to effects that length of court-imposed sentences, gang-related activities in prison, and prison infractions have on time served.

Although these and other issues deserve research attention, we believe that understanding why recidivism indicators more often work against minorities has a particularly high priority. The system is moving to heavier reliance on these indicators precisely to render sentencing and parole decisions more objective. Paradoxically, just the opposite may result if, as we suspect, some of these indicators overlap with race in ways largely unrelated to recidivism.

Definitive policy recommendations will not be possible until some of these research tasks are completed, but three interim policy initiatives may be useful:

- Police and prosecutors should take into account the obstacles to filing charges after minority arrests, particularly the problems with witnesses, and try to find ways of ensuring that pre-arrest identifications will hold firm.
- Plea bargaining needs close monitoring, perhaps by a single deputy, for indications that minority defendants are consistently offered less attractive bargains than whites.
- Until the quality and predictive weight of recidivism indicators can be tested, probation officers, judges, and parole boards should give more weight to indicators of personal cul-

pability than to indicators based on group classifications, such as education and family status.

Although this study shows that minorities are treated differently at a few points in the criminal justice system, it has not found evidence that this results from widespread and consistent racial prejudice in the system. Racial disparities seem to have developed because procedures were adopted without systematic attempts to find out whether they might affect different races differently. Consequently, future research and policy should be concerned with looking behind the scenes at the key actors in the system and their decisionmaking process, primarily at the kind of information they use, how valid it is, and whether its use affects particular racial groups unfairly.

II. BACKGROUND, DATA, AND METHODOLOGY

BACKGROUND

The criminal justice system allows policemen, prosecutors, judges, and parole boards a great deal of discretion in handling most criminal cases. The resulting statistics on minorities in prison have convinced many people that this discretion leads to discrimination. Figure S.1 provides a provocative insight into this issue. Looking at the four top crimes, we find little disparity between the percentage of blacks arrested and the percentage serving prison terms for the crime. These figures suggest that between arrest and sentencing, at any rate, the criminal justice system is simply reacting to the relative number of blacks in the arrest population; however, these violent crimes allow agents of the system less discretion in handling or sentencing. When the crime is murder, forcible rape, robbery, or aggravated assault, a judge has less latitude in deciding about probation or sentence length, or whether the sentence will be served in jail or prison—no matter what color a man is.

Disparity crops up when we move down to lesser crimes. The most striking example is larceny: Blacks account for only 30 percent of the arrest population, but for 51 percent of those serving time for larceny. Why the disparity? One explanation may be that judges can exercise more discretion in dealing with offenders convicted of lesser crimes. If so, the numbers lend some credibility to the charge that discretion leads to discrimination.

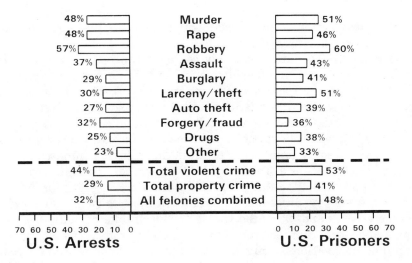

Fig. S.1—Black percentage of arrests and of prison population

Social science researchers have repeatedly addressed this issue, but for every study that finds discrimination, another refutes it. The reasons are various: limited data bases, inability to examine pre-arrest and post-sentencing experiences of offenders, and failure to control for other significant variables.

METHODOLOGY AND STUDY DATA

As described in Sec. I under "Methodology and Data," this study had the advantage of two rich data bases: the OBTS (Offender-Based Transaction Statistics) in California for 1980, and correctional records of prisoners who participated in the RIS (Rand Inmate Survey), which was also the source of the self-reports. This information allowed us to analyze offender behavior and system decisionmaking from crime commission through release from prison.

The OBTS is a computerized information system maintained by the California Bureau of Criminal Statistics. It tracks offenders from point of entry into the criminal justice system to the point of sentencing (or presentencing release). The data cover dispositions that occur in a given year resulting from adult felony arrests made in that year or previous years. Once an offender enters the system, a number of social and legal variables are recorded: sex, race, age, prior record, criminal status, and the original arrest offense. The OBTS also records the date of arrest and offense, conviction offense, date and point of disposition, type of proceeding, type of final sentence, and length of prison sentence.

With the OBTS data, the study could not only track racial differences in case disposition from arrest to sentencing, but could also control for factors such as type of crime and prior record. Both of these factors are essential in understanding whether severity of sentence in *average* statistics indicates racial discrimination.

The RIS consists of data obtained from a self-administered questionnaire completed by approximately 1380 male prison inmates in California, Michigan, and Texas in 1978. Together, these three states house 22 percent of the national population of state prisons. In each state, the survey procedures produced a sample of inmates whose characteristics approximated the statewide intake of male prisoners. The self-reports elicited information about inmates' crimes, arrests, criminal motivations, drug and alcohol use, prior criminal record, prison experience, and the like.

Because self-reports inevitably raise questions about the respondents' veracity, the survey was constructed to allow for both internal and external checks on validity. The questionnaire included pairs of questions, widely separated, that asked for essentially the same information about crimes the respondents had committed and about other topics. This made it possible to check for internal quality (inconsistency, omission, and confusion). Over 83 percent of the respondents filled out the questionnaire accurately, completely, and consistently. The responses were not anonymous, and the official records served not only as part of the analysis but also as an external check on the validity of the self-reports. Although the external check revealed more inconsistencies than the internal check, 59 percent of the respondents had an external error rate of less than 20 percent. However, for most disparities, the records were as questionable as the respondents' veracity. Records are often missing or incomplete, through no fault of the prisoners.

The cross-checking capability also permitted comparisons between inmate characteristics and the quality of the self-reports. One might suspect that some types of people would be less truthful than others. However, an earlier Rand study using the same data found that, with minor exceptions, such individual characteristics as conviction crime, self-image, activity in fraud or "illegal cons," and sociodemographic characteristics, were unrelated to the quality and validity of the response. It also showed no racial differences in validity based on external checks. However, the self-reports of black respondents had lower internal quality than whites' or Hispanics' reports, primarily because of inconsistency and confusion rather than omissions (Chaiken and Chaiken, 1982).

The RIS data permitted us to examine racial differences in crime commission rates—as opposed to arrest rates—and the probability of arrest. This information gave the study a considerable edge over much prior research because it provided a standard for assessing charges that minorities are overarrested. It also enabled us to examine questions of discrimination in corrections and length of sentence served, and of racial differences in crime motivation, weapon use, and in-prison behavior.

III. MAJOR FINDINGS

As Table S.1 indicated, we found some racial differences in the criminal justice system's *handling* of offenders, but few statistically significant racial differences in *criminal behavior*. However, strong trends in some of the data raise important issues for policy and future research.

CASE PROCESSING: ARREST THROUGH SENTENCING

Each year, more than 1.5 million adults in the United States enter the felony disposition process. This process, beginning with an arrest and ending with release or sentencing, is the heart of the criminal justice system. Although a great many people enter the process, very few remain at the end: About 30 percent are dismissed before the preliminary hearing; less than half of those who go to court are convicted; and less than 5 percent of those convicted are sentenced to prison (Greenwood, 1982).

Analysis of the OBTS Data

As for racial differences in the disposition process, the OBTS data revealed an interesting pattern in California. As Table S.2 shows, at the front end of the process, the system seems to treat white offenders more severely and minority offenders more "leniently"; at the back end, the reverse is true.

White suspects are somewhat more likely than minority suspects to be arrested on warrant, and considerably less likely to be released without charges. Whites are also more likely than blacks or Hispanics to have felony charges filed. However, a greater percentage of whites

Table S.2

RACIAL DIFFERENCES IN CASE PROCESSING

Stage	Percentage at Each Stage[a]		
	White	Black	Hispanic
Arrested "on warrant"	9	6	6
Arrested "on view"	91	94	94
Released without charges	20	32	27
Felony charges filed	38	35	35
Misdemeanor charges filed	41	33	37
Felony convictions	20	20	19
Convicted by plea bargain	92	85	87
Tried by jury	7	12	11
Sentenced to probation	21	15	12
Sentenced to prison	6	8	7

[a]SOURCE: OBTS data for 1980.

arrested on felony charges are subsequently charged with misdemeanors, while blacks and Hispanics are less likely to have the seriousness of their cases thus reduced.

Once charged, offenders of all races have about the same chance of being convicted of a felony, but white defendants are more likely than minorities to be convicted by plea bargain. In contrast, minority defendants are more likely than whites to have their felony cases tried by jury. Although plea bargaining, by definition, ensures conviction, it also ensures a reduced charge or a lighter sentence, or both. Moreover, prior research indicates that defendants receive harsher sentences after conviction by juries. These differences may contribute to the racial difference in sentencing. The study found that after a misdemeanor conviction, white defendants had a greater chance than minority defendants of getting probation instead of jail. After a felony conviction, minority defendants were somewhat more likely to get prison instead of jail sentences.

These aggregate findings treat all felonies as if they were the same. If minority defendants had committed more serious felony offenses and had more serious prior records, we would expect their treatment to be more severe. Actually, minorities in the 1980 OBTS did have more serious prior records; a greater proportion of them had been charged with violent crime; and a greater number were on probation or parole. However, by controlling for these factors using multiple regression techniques, we determined that the racial differences in post-arrest and sentencing treatment still held.[1] White arrestees were more likely than minorities to be officially charged following arrest. Black arrestees were more likely to have their cases dismissed by either police or prosecutor. After charges were filed, the conviction rates were similar across the races, but 4 percent more black defendants than whites or Hispanics were sentenced to prison.

Analysis of Court-Imposed Sentence Using RIS Data

Although the scope of our study and our data did not permit us to analyze case processing in all three of the RIS states, it did allow us to compare data on length of court-imposed sentences. And we preferred to use data that would yield findings on possible racial disparities in three states rather than only one. Regression analyses for each state revealed that minorities do receive longer sentences. Controlling for defendant's age, conviction crime, and prior record, we found that minority status alone accounted for 1 to 7 additional months in court-imposed sentences—relative to sentences imposed on white defendants.

CORRECTIONS AND LENGTH OF SENTENCE SERVED

From arrest to sentencing, the system duly records most major decisions involving offenders. Consequently, it is rather easy to see racial differences in handling. However, once a person is sentenced to prison, he is potentially subject to a range of decisions that are not systematically recorded. Prison guards and staff make decisions that strongly influence the quality of an offender's time in prison, and parole boards and other corrections officials decide how long that time lasts. The possibility of discrimination enters into all these decisions, but length of time served is the only one certain to be recorded. In

---

[1]Previous research using the OBTS file has shown significant differences in the processing of defendants from different counties and arrested for different crimes. Consequently, for the regression analysis, we wanted a sample from the same county and charged with the same crime. We were able to obtain a large homogeneous sample (n=6652) by selecting defendants who were charged with robbery in Los Angeles County in 1980.

other words, corrections is a closed world in which discrimination could flourish.

That charge has frequently been brought against the system, and the steady increase of prison racial problems makes it imperative to examine the treatment that different races receive in prison and at parole. We examined prison treatment and length of sentence served using the RIS and the official records of our sample, where available. Our analysis revealed some racial differences for participation in work and treatment programs, but they were largely determined by the prisoners, not by guards or staff.

To create a larger framework for assessing possible discrimination, the study established criteria for identifying inmates who needed education, vocational training, and alcohol and drug treatment programs. We then compared the percentage who had need with with the percentage that participated for each racial group.

Although there were no significant racial differences in the overall rate of program participation, there were some differences in participation, relative to need. In all three states, participation matched need most closely for education. In all three states, a greater percentage of minorities than of whites were identified as having high need for education. However, in Texas, blacks received significantly less education treatment. Moreover in two of the study states, blacks had a significantly higher need for vocational training than whites or Hispanics, but did not have significantly higher participation rates. Compared with the other racial groups, blacks who needed alcohol treatment had a significantly lower participation rate.

Nevertheless, the reasons respondents gave for *not participating* suggested that minorities were discriminating against the programs, not vice versa. Prisoners most often said they were "too busy" or "didn't need" to participate; few said that they did not participate because staff discouraged them. The findings for work assignments were similar.

We found, however, that although minorities received roughly equal treatment in prison, race consistently made a difference when it came time for release. In Texas, blacks and Hispanics consistently served longer time than whites—and the disparity was appreciably larger than the disparity in court-imposed sentences. In California, blacks served slightly longer sentences, but the disparity largely reflected the original sentencing differences. In Michigan, the parole process evidently worked in favor of blacks. Although their court-imposed sentences were considerably longer than those of whites, they did not actually serve longer (see Table S.3).

Table S.3

ADDITIONAL MONTHS IMPOSED AND SERVED FOR MINORITIES

State	Court-imposed sentence	Time Served
California		
Blacks	+1.4 months	+2.4 months*
Hispanics	+6.5 months*	+5.0 months*
Michigan		
Blacks	+7.2 months*	1.7 months
Hispanics	(small sample)	(small sample)
Texas		
Blacks	+3.7 months	+7.7 months*
Hispanics	+2.0 months	+8.1 months*

*Statistically significant.

CRIME COMMISSION RATES AND PROBABILITY OF ARREST

To estimate whether minorities are overarrested, *relative to the number of crimes they actually commit,* analysts need comparable "pre-arrest" information—variety of crimes committed, incidence of crime or crime commission rates, and the probability of arrest—for white and minority arrestees. Although official records provide information on the crimes for which offenders are arrested and convicted, they provide no information on how many other crimes and types of crimes these people commit. To overcome this problem, we used data from the RIS on the actual types and number of crimes that offenders reported committing in the 15-month period preceding their current imprisonment. Inmates also reported on the number of arrests for each kind of crime they had committed during the same period. Using this information, we estimated each offender's annualized crime rate. Our purpose was to estimate separately the range of crime types in the different racial groups, the crime-commission rates for individuals in those groups, and then to estimate the probability that a single crime would result in arrest for members of that group. We found strong evidence that *in proportion to the kind and amount of crime they commit*, minorities are not being overarrested.[2]

There are racial differences in the range of crime *types* committed:

- More Hispanics reported committing personal crimes—both personal robberies and aggravated assault.
- More whites and Hispanics reported involvement in both drug dealing and burglary.
- Significantly more whites committed forgery and credit card and auto thefts.

We found few consistent, statistically significant, differences in *crime commission rates* among the racial groups. However, there were differences in rates for two particular crimes.

- Blacks reported committing fewer burglaries than whites or Hispanics.
- Hispanics reported fewer frauds and swindles than whites or blacks.
- Black and white offenders reported almost identical rates of robberies, grand larcenies, and auto thefts.
- Black and white offenders were involved in more drug deals than Hispanics, but the differences were not statistically significant.

That last finding illustrates the difference between range of criminality and incidence of crime. The findings on range indicate that more Hispanics than blacks reported being involved in at least one drug deal. However, the annualized crime rates, which represent incidence, indicate that once involved in drug dealing, blacks committed more of it than Hispanics did.

Even though minorities are not overarrested relative to the number of crimes they commit, it is still possible that they have a higher *probability* than whites of being arrested for those crimes. Critics of the system have argued that this explains why blacks are "overrepresented" in the arrest and prison populations. We found, however, that the probability of being arrested for a crime is extremely low regardless of race. For example, only 6 percent of the burglaries, 21 percent of the business robberies, 5 percent of the forgeries, and less than 1 percent of the drug sales reported by these offenders resulted in ar-

---

[2]The RIS has certain limitations as a means of calculating crime rates and of detecting racial differences in these rates. All the respondents were in prison and the sample was chosen to represent each state's male prison population. Therefore, it is not appropriate to view these crime rates as applicable to offenders in the community. They refer only to a cohort of incoming prisoners in the states chosen for this study. Selection effects and other factors cause these rates to be substantially higher than those for "typical" offenders (Rolph, Chaiken, and Houchens, 1981).

rest. This finding held for all racial groups. We found no statistically significant racial differences in arrest probability for the crimes we studied with the exception of personal robbery. For personal robbery, blacks and Hispanics did report suffering more arrests relative to the number of crimes they committed.

MOTIVATION, WEAPON USE, AND PRISON BEHAVIOR

Motivation, weapon use, and prison behavior seem likely to influence the impression a prisoner makes on probation officers, judges, and parole boards. Using RIS data, we examined these characteristics for racial differences that might help explain the differences we observed in sentencing and time served. The statistically significant differences were few and not very helpful in explaining those decisions.

All three racial groups rated economic distress as the primary motive for committing crime, with "high times" second and "temper" third. However, there was only one statistically significant difference in motivation: Whites rated "high times" much higher than blacks and Hispanics did. Nevertheless, there were some other, suggestive, differences. Blacks rated economic distress considerably higher than high times, while whites rated it only slightly higher. This suggests that socioeconomic conditions among blacks may be more consistently related to crime than they are among whites. That comes as no particular surprise; but if probation officers, judges, and parole boards see unemployment as an indicator of recidivism—rather than as a mitigating circumstance in crime—blacks or any unemployed offenders are likely to receive harsher sentences and serve longer.

In weapons use, the data revealed a few clear racial differences, but if those differences influence sentencing or parole decisions, they do so inconsistently. Hispanics are more likely than whites to be sent to prison and to stay there longer, and Hispanics show a statistically significant preference for using knives in all crimes. Moreover, they indicated a greater tendency to seriously injure their victims. In contrast, the proportion of blacks in prison for burglary is considerably higher than the proportion of blacks arrested for that crime (see Fig. S.1). Yet, in our sample, blacks were the least likely to be armed during burglaries. Indeed, they were less likely than whites to use guns and less likely than Hispanics to use knives. If these differences indicate that blacks are less violent and, perhaps, less "professional" than the other groups, probation officers and judges apparently do not recognize it. Our findings on prison violence raise similarly conflicting suggestions.

The percentage of inmates with behavioral infractions differs markedly across states—significantly for five of the seven infraction types we studied. We therefore examined each state separately. Racial differences were pronounced for prison behavior. However, in all three states, age was most strongly, and negatively, correlated with higher infractions. Younger prisoners in all three states got into the most trouble. After age came race, but not consistently for all states. In California, white inmates had the highest infraction rate; in Texas, blacks did. The high-rate infractors had the following profiles:

- California: a young white inmate who has had limited exposure to treatment programs, and who currently has no prison work assignment.
- Michigan: A young inmate serving for nonviolent crime.
- Texas: A young black inmate with few serious convictions, who has had limited exposure to treatment programs and currently has no prison work assignment.

Racial differences in prison behavior had no apparent relation to length of sentence served. In California, whites have significantly higher infraction rates than blacks. In Texas, the reverse is true. Yet, in both states, blacks serve longer sentences. (In Michigan, where there were no statistically significant racial differences in prison behavior, race also had no bearing on length of time served.)

Having looked at the criminal justice system's treatment of offenders and at offenders' behavior, we have still been unable to account for racial differences in post-arrest release rates, in sentencing, and in some portion of time served. Section IV presents some conclusions drawn from our findings and from other research that may explain these differences.

IV. CONCLUSIONS OF THE STUDY

We again advise the reader that, whenever the data were sufficient to do so, our analyses of system decisions and criminal behavior controlled for the most obvious variables that could reasonably account for apparent racial differences. In these comparisons, then, our offenders are rather "interchangeable" except for race. We also want to stress again that both our findings and our conclusions reflect data from only three states. Further, our self-report data come from prisoners, and conclusions drawn from those data are not applicable to the criminal population at large.

EXPLAINING DISPARITIES IN CASE PROCESSING AND TIME SERVED

At most major decision points, the criminal justice system does not discriminate against minorities. However, race does affect post-arrest release, length and type of sentence imposed, and length of sentence served.

Our analysis of the RIS data found that minorities are not over-represented in the arrest population, *relative to the number of crimes they actually commit*, nor are they more likely than whites to be arrested for those crimes. Nevertheless, the OBTS analysis raised a question that the study could not answer: If blacks and Hispanics are not being overarrested, why are police and prosecutors so much more likely to let them go without filing charges? One possibility is that the police more often arrest minorities on "probable-cause" evidence that subsequently fails to meet the filing standard of "evidence beyond a reasonable doubt."

Prior research may shed some light on this phenomenon. Earlier studies have shown that arrests depend heavily on witnesses' or victims' identifying or carefully describing the suspect (Greenwood, Petersilia, Chaiken, 1978). Prosecutors may have a more difficult time making cases against minorities "beyond a reasonable doubt" because of problems with victim and witness identifications. Frequently, witnesses or victims who were supportive at the arrest stage become less cooperative as the case proceeds:

- White witnesses and victims appear to have a harder time making positive identifications of minority suspects than of white suspects.
- Crimes against minority victims are most often committed by minority suspects, often acquaintances. After the arrest, victims frequently refuse to prosecute, withdraw the identification, or refuse to testify.
- Witnesses also become uncooperative if they have been intimidated or feel threatened by the defendant or by aspects of the criminal justice system.
- A major factor distinguishing cooperative from uncooperative witnesses is simple confusion about where they are supposed to appear or about what they are supposed to do when they get there.

In addition to "evidentiary" problems, the study found another racial difference in case processing that may help explain a small proportion of the high release rates for minorities. A slightly higher percentage of white suspects than blacks were arrested with a warrant in the study period. Because the criteria for issuing warrants are essentially the same as the criteria for filing criminal charges, cases involving warrants would be less likely to develop evidentiary problems after arrest. However, there is only a 3 percentage point difference between whites and minorities for warrant arrests.

Nevertheless, this difference raises a provocative question: Why are the police apparently more hesitant to arrest white than minority suspects without a warrant? From the release rates, it appears that the police and prosecutors have a harder time making a "filable" case against minorities. Yet, by getting warrants more often to arrest whites, the police implicitly indicate that the reverse is true. Or, they may assume that minority suspects are less likely than white suspects to make false arrest charges or other kinds of trouble if a case is not filed.

Whatever their reasons, the racial differences in warrant arrests and release rates suggest that the police operate on different assumptions about minorities than about whites when they make arrests. Other study findings tend to reinforce the suggestion that the system regards minorities differently. Controlling for the factors most likely to influence sentencing and parole decisions, the analysis still found that blacks and Hispanics are less likely to be given probation, more likely to receive *prison* sentences, more likely to receive longer sentences, and more likely to serve longer time.

As Fig. S.1 showed, for very serious crimes, blacks are represented about equally in the arrest and prison populations. In other words, the prevalence of these crimes among blacks primarily dictates their numbers in the prison population. However, as we move to property crimes, the disparity between blacks' proportions of the arrest and prison populations widens considerably. This disparity suggests that probation officers, judges, and parole boards are exercising discretion in sentencing and/or release decisions in ways that result in *de facto* discrimination against blacks. The same is true for Hispanics, who serve even longer time than blacks.

Possibly, the racial differences in type and length of sentence imposed reflect racial differences in plea bargaining and jury trials. Fully 92 percent of white defendants were convicted by plea bargaining, compared with 85 percent for blacks and 87 percent for Hispanics. Those numbers imply the percentage that engaged in plea bargaining —since, by nature, plea bargaining virtually ensures conviction. However, it also virtually guarantees a reduced charge and/or lighter sentencing. Defendants who go to trial generally receive harsher sentences, and our study found that only 7 percent of whites prosecuted in Superior Court were tried by jury, compared with 12 percent for blacks and 11 percent for Hispanics.

However, even if these mechanisms did account for the apparent racial differences in sentencing, the implication of bias simply shifts to another node in the system. Why should minorities plea bargain less and go to jury trial more than whites? If the differences represent defendants' attitudes and decisions, then the system is not actively responsible for this racial difference. If these differences reflect decisions by prosecutors or decisions by default, then the issue of bias returns. And it may reflect the kind of differences that are implied by the prefiling release rates for minorities.

The suggestion that the system regards whites and minorities differently may enter into sentencing in another way. Judges may hesitate to send white defendants to prison for two reasons. First, research indicates that in prisons where whites are the minority, they are often victimized by the dominant racial group, whether black or Hispanic. (In most states, blacks now outnumber whites in the prison population.) Second, judges may regard whites as better candidates for rehabilitation.

Research on sentence patterns supports the implication that the system "values" whites more than it does minorities. For example, Zimring, Eigen, and O'Malley (1976) found that blacks who kill whites receive life imprisonment or the death sentence more than twice as often as when they kill blacks. Other research has tended to bear out this relationship for other crimes as well: Defendants get harsher sentences if the victim is white than if he is black.

INFORMATION USED IN SENTENCING AND PAROLE

Putting aside the ambiguity of findings about post-arrest release, the study found strong racial differences only in length and type of sentence imposed and length of time served. If there is discrimination in the system, it is inconsistent. Minorities are no more likely than whites to be arrested or convicted of crimes nor to be treated differently by corrections. Yet, they are given longer, harsher sentences at conviction, and wind up serving longer terms than whites in two of our study states. It may be possible to explain these inconsistencies by considering who makes decisions at key points in the system and what kinds of information they use to make those decisions.

As the accused moves through the system, more information about him is attached to his folder and that information is weighted differentially. Police and prosecutors are primarily concerned with "just deserts." Their legal mission is to ensure that criminals are convicted. They concentrate on the information they need to make arrest and conviction stick—primarily information about the crime and about the offender's prior record—according to strict legal rules. Judges also consider the nature of the crime and prior record in weighing just deserts, but they are further concerned with the defendant's potential for rehabilitation or recidivism. In other words, will returning him to society through probation or a lighter sentence endanger society? In deciding on probation, jail, or prison for an offender, they consider his conviction crime, prior record, *and* his personal and socioeconomic characteristics.

To provide the latter material, probation officers in most counties prepare a presentence investigation report (PSR), which contains a sentence recommendation. Probation officers are more concerned with analyzing and understanding the person and his situation, and they tend to deemphasize the legal technicalities necessary to assess guilt and convictability. The PSR describes the subject's family background, marital status, education and employment history, past encounters with the law, gang affiliation, drug and alcohol use, etc. In most states, it is the key document in sentencing and parole decisions. Its recommendations are generally followed by the sentencing judge, and its characterization of the defendant becomes the core of the parole board's case-summary file.

The influence of the PSR may help explain the racial differences in sentencing and time served: Minorities often do not show up well in PSR indicators of recidivism, such as family instability and unemployment. As a result, probation officers, judges, and parole boards are often impelled to identify minorities as higher risks.

These conjectures are supported by the comparison between length of sentence imposed and time served. In California, determinate sentencing practices make length of time served depend primarily on length of sentence imposed. Thus, racial differences in time served there, especially for Hispanics, reflect racial disparities in sentencing. Minority defendants also receive longer sentences than whites in Texas, and parole decisions there lengthen those sentences even more, relative to time served by whites. In Michigan, we found a reverse effect. Blacks received sentences 7.2 months longer than white defendants, but they served roughly equal time.

This contrast can perhaps be explained by the parole practices in Texas and Michigan. Texas has a very individualized, highly discretionary, parole process that incorporates the full range of an inmate's criminal history and personal and socioeconomic characteristics. Since 1976, Michigan parole decisions have been based almost exclusively on legal indicators of personal culpability, e.g., juvenile record, violence of conviction crime, and prison behavior. Evidently, this practice not only overcomes racial disparities in time served, but also even overcomes racial disparities in sentencing. Nevertheless, overcoming racial disparities in sentencing is not the primary, nor perhaps the proper, concern of parole boards. Their major responsibility is to decide whether an inmate can safely be returned to society. By putting aside the socioeconomic and other extra-legal indicators of recidivism, they may be setting potential recidivists loose.

ASSESSING THE INDICATORS OF RECIDIVISM

If the indicators of recidivism are valid, the criminal justice system is not discriminating against minorities in its sentencing and parole decisions; it is simply reflecting the larger racial problems of society. However, our research suggests that the indicators may be less objective (and certainly less "race-neutral") than past research and practice have indicated.

The overrepresentation of minorities in aggregate arrest statistics has tended to obscure the fact that the criminal justice system and criminal justice research are, nevertheless, dealing with a criminal population that is half white and half minority. Unless minorities in *that* population have had higher recidivism rates than whites, there is no reason why minorities should consistently be seen as presenting a higher risk of recidivism. There is clearly a much higher *prevalence* of crime within the minority portion of the national population—that prevalence largely accounts for their equal representation with whites in the criminal population. But there is no evidence that they have a higher recidivism rate.

The RIS data indicate that, once involved in crime, whites and minorities in the sample had virtually the same annual crime commission rates. This accords with Blumstein and Graddy's (1981) finding that the recidivism rate for index offenses is approximately 0.85 *for both whites and nonwhites*. Thus, the data suggest that large racial differences in aggregate arrest rates must be attributed primarily to differences in *ever becoming involved in crime at all* and not to different patterns among those who do participate.

Under these circumstances, any empirically derived indicators of recidivism should target a roughly equal number of whites and minorities. The reason this does not happen may be the relative sizes and diversity of the base populations. The black portion of the criminal population draws from a population base that is much smaller and more homogeneous, socioeconomically and culturally. That is, black criminals are more likely than their white counterparts to have common socioeconomic and cultural characteristics. The white half of the criminal population comes from a vastly larger, more heterogeneous base. Individuals in it are motivated variously, and come from many different cultural, ethnic, and economic backgrounds. Consequently, the characteristics associated with "black criminality" are more consistent, more visible, and more "countable" than those associated with white criminality. Moreover, because *prevalence* of crime is so much higher than incidence of crime (or recidivism) among minorities, characteristics associated with prevalence of crime among blacks (e.g., unemployment, family instability) may overwhelm indicators of prevalence for the entire criminal population. They may also mask indicators of recidivism common to both blacks and whites.

The findings on criminal motivation and economic need lend support to this hypothesis. Blacks rated economic distress much higher than "high times" and very much higher than "temper" as their motive for committing crime. They also rated it more highly than either whites or Hispanics did. Moreover, the black inmates were consistently identified as economically distressed by the study's criteria for economic need. These findings imply that socioeconomic characteristics are more consistent and more consistently related to crime among blacks than they are among whites. Considering that blacks make up approximately half of the criminal population, their characteristics may have the same effect on indicators of prevalence and recidivism that the extremely high crime rates of a few individuals have on average crime rates.

This is a real vicious circle: As long as the "black experience" conduces to crime, blacks will be identified as potential recidivists, will serve prison terms instead of jail terms, will serve longer time, and will thus be identified as more serious criminals.

V. IMPLICATIONS FOR FUTURE RESEARCH AND POLICY

These findings and conclusions raise some compelling issues for criminal justice research and policy. The first priority for both will be to examine the indicators used in sentencing and parole decisions.

QUESTIONS FOR FUTURE RESEARCH

Assessing the Indicators of Recidivism

The criminal justice system is moving toward greater use of prediction tables that measure an offender's risk of recidivism. These tables are based on the actuarially determined risk associated with factors such as prior record, employment, and education. This "categoric risk" technique does not assume that the facts of each case are unique. Rather, it assumes that the risk of recidivism is distributed fairly uniformly among groups of individuals who share certain characteristics.

According to some experts, adopting this more objective technique reduces racial disparities because it severely limits discretion and because the indicators are racially neutral. However, as we argued in Sec. IV, these indicators may appear racially neutral, but in practice they may overlap with racial status. Using factors that correlate highly with race will have the same effect as using race itself as an indicator.

We need to reexamine the statistical methods and the evidence used to develop these risk prediction schemes. The minority half of the criminal population probably has more characteristics in common, especially socioeconomic characteristics, than does the white half. Consequently, these characteristics may statistically overwhelm others that might indicate the risk of recidivism more precisely for both whites and blacks. Analysts will need a methodology that permits them to control for homogeneity in the minority (largely black) half of the criminal population.

If different recidivism indicators can be isolated using that methodology, researchers will then have to determine whether the resulting sentencing standards still lead to harsher treatment for minorities. Assuming that we want a system that can discriminate between high and low probability of recidivism, we also need some standard of judicial review that balances the state's interest in accurate identification of recidivists against the imperative that group classifications should not be implicit race classifications.

For each indicator that has racial links, we need to ask: How much predictive efficiency would the state lose by omitting this indicator from its sentencing standards? Thus framed, the question is not whether prediction tables could (or should) be used, but to what extent the state should sacrifice a degree of predictive efficiency to racial equity. Obviously, characteristics showing personal culpability (for example, prior convictions) should always be seen as acceptable factors for assessing risk. Even if minorities have a disproportionate number of them, these characteristics indicate individual, not group, status.

Post-Arrest Release Rates and Evidentiary Problems

Racial differences in post-arrest release rates should be explored. The RIS data show that the police are not simply overarresting minorities, relative to the crimes they commit, and then having to let them go. However, our findings do not discount the charge that the police arrest minorities on weaker evidence. Nevertheless, previous research suggests that the bulk of cases dismissed before filing involved uncooperative victims, and other research has suggested that minority cases more often have problems with victims and witnesses. Future research could inquire why so many victims become uncooperative, whether the reasons differ in minority cases, and how often either the suspect or the criminal justice system itself intimidates victims or witnesses.

Racial Differences in Plea Bargaining and Sentence Severity

This study did not control for plea bargaining in analyzing racial differences in sentence severity. If future research establishes that plea bargaining contributes to those differences, the next important research task would be to discover why minority defendants are less likely than whites to plea bargain and more likely to have jury trials. Do prosecutors consistently offer less attractive plea bargains to minority defendants, or do minority defendants simply insist more on jury trials?

Effect of Prisons' Racial Mix on Sentencing

If judges are increasingly reluctant to send white offenders to prisons where blacks and Hispanics outnumber them, racial differences in sentence severity will widen, and the disproportion of minorities in prison will grow. This sensitive issue will not be easy to resolve empirically. The first task would be to establish that judges are indeed influenced by reports that white prisoners are often victimized. The second task would be to establish whether these reports are valid; if they are, the criminal justice system will face harder issues than sentencing practices. Among the most serious might be pressure for segregated facilities.

How Prison-Gang Membership Affects Length of Sentence Served

We need to understand how gang-related activities affect length of sentence served and participation in prison treatment and work programs. In California, one out of every seven prisoners is currently held in administrative segregation, most of them for gang-related activities, and a greater proportion of the black and Hispanic inmates admit to gang membership. A greater proportion of minorities may be in segregation because of gang affiliation, and inmates in segregation may have restricted access to prison treatment and work programs. Since program participation affects release decisions, gang affiliation may contribute significantly to racial differences in time served.

The Prison Environment's Influence on In-Prison Behavior

Some inmates, predicted to be high infractors, exhibited rather exemplary behavior. To what extent can their good behavior be attributed to characteristics of the institution, e.g., specific security measures, inmate-to-staff ratio, recreational facilities, the total size of the institution, housing arrangements, and so forth?

The Connection Between Prison Violence and Idleness

Prison administrators face both rising violence and shrinking budgets. Research can help them cope by finding out more about the relationship between idleness and prison violence and identifying the kinds of inmates whose participation in programs will bring about the greatest reduction in violence.

POLICY RECOMMENDATIONS

Definitive policy recommendations must await findings from some of these research studies, but we can recommend some interim policy initiatives.

(1) *Police and prosecutors need to be more aware of the difficulty of getting adequate evidence with which to convict minority suspects.* The high release rates for minorities suggest that minority suspects are not as likely as whites to be identified from lineups or elsewhere, and that victims or key witnesses in minority cases often prove uncoopera-

tive after the arrest has taken place. Police and prosecutors may need to work harder at securing the trust and cooperation of minority victims and witnesses.

(2) *The plea bargaining process needs to be closely monitored for any indications that minorities are offered less attractive plea bargains than those offered to whites.* One way to assure greater uniformity is to have a single deputy review all the plea negotiations. Moreover, minorities' unfamiliarity with and distrust of the system may cause them to insist on a trial. If so, they should be informed that sentences resulting from jury trials are generally more severe.

(3) *Judges and probation officers must begin to distinguish between information concerning the defendant's personal culpability and information that reflects his social status.* The latter information may not be as racially neutral or objective as previous research has indicated. Until the indicators of recidivism have been reanalyzed, we recommend that officials weight the criminal's characteristics more heavily than socioeconomic indicators in sentencing and parole decisions.

(4) *To reduce prison violence, prison administrators should allocate work and treatment programs, particularly prison jobs, to younger inmates, who are responsible for most prison violence.*

(5) Finally, *we recommend another look at rehabilitation.* It is perhaps unfashionable to talk about rehabilitation when prison administrators are faced with shrinking budgets, increased population, and more fractious inmates. In this context, most administrators have been forced to assign low priorities to treatment programs. Although rehabilitation programs have not yet lived up to expectations, the implications of this trend are troubling. The RIS data indicated that most inmates do not get the treatment that they need. Two-thirds of the inmates who were chronically unemployed preceding their imprisonment failed to participate in vocational training programs. Two-thirds of those with alcohol problems did not receive alcohol treatment. And about 95 percent of those with drug problems did not get drug treatment in Texas and California.[1] Most inmates reported that they failed to participate in programs because they "didn't have time" or "didn't need" them. Drug treatment was the exception. About one-third of the inmates who needed drug treatment said they were not in drug programs because no programs were available. This is especially distressing, because over half of those who did participate in a drug program believed it had benefitted them and that it had reduced their likelihood of returning to crime after release.

Like other public institutions, the criminal justice system faces growing economic restrictions. It has had to make hard choices among

---

[1] In Michigan, about half of the drug-dependent inmates received treatment.

policies, programs, and research priorities. However, we believe that there could be no more important priority for policy and research than attempting to identify those aspects of the system that permit harsher treatment of minorities.

This study leaves us with guarded optimism concerning the system and the personnel who operate it. We did not find widespread, conscious prejudice against certain racial groups. Instead, what racial disparities we found seem to be due to the system's adopting procedures without analyzing their possible effects on different racial groups. Criminal justice research and policy now need to look behind the scenes. They need to focus on the key actors and their decision-making: what information they use, how accurate it is, and whether its imposition affects particular racial groups unfairly.

ACKNOWLEDGMENTS

Foremost, my sincere appreciation goes to Joyce Peterson, a Communications Analyst in Rand's Publications Department. Her helpfulness in forging the preliminary draft into its final form cannot be overstated.

Appreciation must also be extended to the hundreds of inmates willing to involve themselves in this study. They participated in numerous pretest sessions and in the final sample. It appears they responded candidly about themselves, their crimes, their treatment needs, and their prison experiences. Without their willingness to share this information, parts of this study could not have been undertaken.

This research required the extensive cooperation of prison officials in California, Michigan, and Texas. My gratitude is extended to Perry Johnson (Michigan), W. J. Estelle, Jr. (Texas), and Jiro Enomoto (formerly of California). James M. Watson and James Rasmussen, Bureau of Criminal Statistics, were most generous in providing us with California's OBTS data for 1980.

Allen Breed, the former Director of the National Institute of Corrections, Department of Justice, provided the opportunity to pursue this research. Special thanks also go to Larry Soloman and Robert Smith, Assistant Directors, and John Wallace and Phyllis Modley, our grant monitors, for their sustained encouragement.

Many persons reviewed drafts of this report and made insightful suggestions concerning the analysis, presentation, and conclusions. They include: Abe Chavez, Alfred Blumstein, Cy Shain, Lowell Jensen, Maxine Singer, Nathaniel Trives, Rose Matsui Ochi, Lincoln Fortson, Horace McFall, Philip Cook, Stevens Clarke, James Q. Wilson, Daniel Glaser, Charles Wellford, Richard Dehais, James Collins, Scott Christianson, Franklin Zimring, Don Gottfredson, and Michael Tonry. Stevens Clarke was especially diligent in his review, and many of his suggestions improved the final product.

Several Rand colleagues aided the research in important ways. Sue Polich organized and operated the information retrieval system that permitted use of data from multiple sources. She also did the programming for the analysis, and gave advice about the appropriateness of the statistical packages used. Dr. Allan Abrahamse and Dr. John Rolph gave statistical advice in planning the multivariate analysis, and in the crime rate and arrest probability analysis. Dr. Stephen Klein's review was most helpful, and several additional analyses were performed as a result of his suggestions. Barbara Williams, Rand's current Criminal Justice Program Director, assisted in administrative matters whenever needed.

CONTENTS

FIGURES

TABLES

I. INTRODUCTION

The U.S. criminal justice system allows policemen, prosecutors, judges, and parole boards a great deal of discretion in handling most criminal cases. The statistics on minorities in prison have convinced many people that this discretion leads to discrimination. These statistics are, indeed, alarming.

As Fig. 1.1 shows, blacks make up only 12 percent of the U.S. population, but 48 percent of the prison population. This seemingly outrageous disparity has prompted allegations that the police overarrest minorities, prosecutors pursue their cases more vigorously, judges sentence them more severely, and corrections officials make sure they stay incarcerated longer than whites. However, it is difficult to believe that discrimination in the United States is so vast as to produce such a disparity. Logic suggests and statistics show that much of this disparity is simply due to the much greater prevalence of crime among minorities than among whites. As Alfred Blumstein (1981) recently concluded, "... racial differences in arrest alone account for the bulk of racial differences in incarceration."

The facts about traditional street crimes support this conclusion. These crimes are more numerous among young people than old, among males than females, among blacks than whites, and among

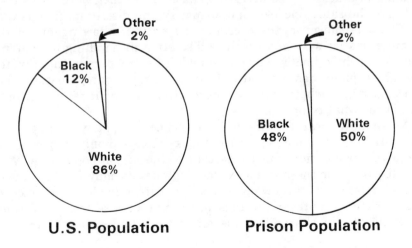

U.S. Population **Prison Population**

Fig. 1.1—Racial distribution in the United States and
the prison population

low-income than high-income people, and are commoner in urban centers than in the country. Moreover, the prototype for both offender and victim is the same: a young, poor, black male ghetto-dweller. An astonishing 51 percent of black males living in large cities are arrested at least once for an index crime during their lives, compared with only 14 percent of white males.[1] Fully 18 percent of black males serve time in prison or jail, either as juveniles or adults, compared with 3 percent of white males (Greenfeld, 1981). Murder is the leading cause of death for young black males, and is almost as high for young black females.

Crime is a fact of life in the ghetto. Blacks and other minorities must cope with both crime and the criminal justice system much more than whites, with devastating effects on families, employment, and self-respect. This situation raises a vital question for criminal justice research. Does the American judicial system worsen the problem by discriminating against minorities in any way? The issue is not whether they commit a disproportionate amount of crime, but whether the criminal justice system compounds the problem by treating them differently from whites.

Figure 1.2 provides a provocative insight into this question. Looking at the four top crimes, we find very little disparity between the percentage of blacks arrested and the percentage serving prison terms for the crimes. These figures suggest that the criminal justice system is behaving largely "reactively" instead of "pro-actively." Between arrest and sentencing, at any rate, it is simply reacting to the relative number of blacks in the arrest population. In other words, this does not give the same impression of disparity and discrimination as that in Fig. 1.1. However, these crimes, by nature, allow agents of the criminal justice system very little discretion in handling or sentencing. When the crime is murder, forcible rape, robbery, or aggravated assault, a judge has less latitude in deciding about probation, sentence length, or whether the sentence will be served in jail or prison— no matter what color a man is.

As we move down the line to lesser crimes, disparity emerges. The most striking example is larceny: Blacks make up only 30 percent of the arrest population, but 51 percent of the prison population. Why the disparity for these crimes? One explanation may be that judges can exercise more discretion in dealing with offenders convicted of these crimes. Whatever the reason, the numbers seem to lend some credibility to the charge that discretion leads to discrimination.

---

[1]Blumstein and Graddy (1981). Index offenses are murder, rape, robbery, assault, burglary, larceny/theft, auto theft, and arson.

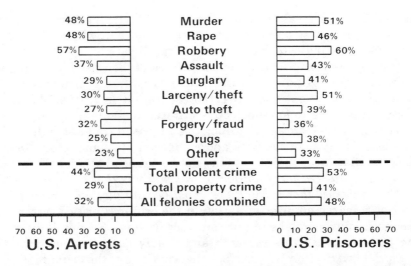

U.S. Arrests		U.S. Prisoners
48%	Murder	51%
48%	Rape	46%
57%	Robbery	60%
37%	Assault	43%
29%	Burglary	41%
30%	Larceny/theft	51%
27%	Auto theft	39%
32%	Forgery/fraud	36%
25%	Drugs	38%
23%	Other	33%
44%	Total violent crime	53%
29%	Total property crime	41%
32%	All felonies combined	48%

Fig. 1.2—Comparison of blacks in arrest and prison population

This study has three objectives:

- To see if there is any evidence that the criminal justice system systematically treats minorities differently from whites;
- If there is such evidence, to see whether that treatment represents discrimination or is simply a reaction to the extent and seriousness of minority crimes; and
- To discuss the policy implications for correcting any bias.

The study relies primarily on two data sources: California's Offender-Based Transaction Statistics (OBTS) for 1980 and the Rand Inmate Survey (RIS). The OBTS is a computerized information system maintained by the California Bureau of Criminal Statistics that tracks the processing of offenders from arrest to sentencing. The RIS consists of data obtained from self-reports of 1380 prison inmates in California, Michigan, and Texas. Together, these data sources provide unique insights into racial differences in the commission of crime and the handling of criminals.

Analysis of the data reveals that at most key decision points in the criminal justice process, minorities in these states are treated the same as whites. However, there is evidence that in sentencing and length of time served, minorities are treated more severely. For the same crime and with similar criminal records, whites are more likely to get probation, to go to jail instead of prison, to receive shorter sentences, and to serve less time behind bars than minority offenders. Paradoxically, this apparent discrimination may arise from conscientious efforts to use "racially neutral" indicators to assess an offender's susceptibility to treatment and the risk of returning him to society. Evidently, minority offenders are more likely than whites to be identified by these indicators as potential "recidivists."

If these indicators identify minorities as higher risks because they do have higher recidivism rates, there is little the criminal justice system can do about their overrepresentation in prison. Worse, as more states move to more objective criteria for sentencing and parole decisions, the percentage of minorities in prison could actually grow. However, analysis of the data and evidence from some prior research suggests that these indicators may not be so racially neutral after all. *A fundamental recommendation of this study is that these indicators, and the analyses that led to them, must be carefully reconsidered.*

Prior research on discrimination in the criminal justice system has produced controversial and contradictory findings. Section II discusses the problems with this research and briefly describes our data and methodology. Section III describes the workings of the criminal justice system and identifies racial differences in case processing revealed in the OBTS data. Section IV analyzes data from the RIS for racial differences in crime commission rates and the probability of being arrested. Section V looks at racial differences following the imposition of a court sentence, specifically participation in prison treatment and work programs and length of sentence actually served. Section VI explores racial differences in offender characteristics, specifically crime motivation, weapon use, and prison violence. Section VII summarizes our findings and conclusions, and draws implications for future research and policy. Appendixes A through D present the regression results.

II. BACKGROUND AND DATA FOR THE STUDY

Ours is not the first study of racial differences in crime and criminal justice processing. The subject has occupied researchers since the early 1900s; but despite the vast amount of energy that has been spent on the subject, few empirically based generalizations can be drawn. The research to date contains numerous contradictions and inconsistencies. Some studies purport to have found evidence of harsher treatment of minorities;[1] others have found reverse discrimination, with minorities treated more leniently than whites in particular cases and particular phases of judicial processing.[2]

What explains such inconsistent research findings? Perhaps foremost is poor methodology. Most of the research uses weak statistical tests and fails to control for confounding variables. For instance, research may show that blacks, once convicted, are more often sentenced to prison than nonblacks; some authors then conclude that the system is racist. Such a conclusion is highly questionable, because the analysis has usually failed to control for other relevant variables. It may be possible, for example, that blacks are sentenced more severely because they commit more serious crimes or because they are more likely to have prior criminal records. Race may also be spuriously related to sanctions because it is related to other "extralegal" attributes of the defendant, such as socioeconomic status, that are themselves strongly related to sanctions.[3] Improved methodological rigor is essential for strengthening the findings in this research area.

Another problem, more fundamental and not as easily rectified as the methodological problem, is the inability of researchers to examine decisionmaking in the nonreviewable stages of the justice process. Previous research has concentrated almost exclusively on system processing from police arrest through imposition of sentence. Researchers usually generate a data base that begins with a sample of persons arrested. That "arrest cohort" is then tracked through to sentencing, where the handling of minority and nonminority persons is

---

[1]Piliavin and Briar (1964); Ferdinand and Luchterhand (1970); Thornberry (1973); Carroll and Mondrick (1976); Gibson (1978). Studies that found no evidence of discrimination include: Terry (1967); Black (1970); Black and Reiss (1970); Greeñ (1970); Hagan (1974); Clarke and Koch (1976, 1980); and Hindelang (1978).

[2]Greenwood et al. (1973); Morris and Tonry (1980); Zimring (1976).

[3]More complete reviews of previous research are contained in the relevant sections of this report.

compared. Those familiar with the system know that these events include only part of the justice system.

Even if methodological rigor were applied to studying those events, one would still not have a grasp of the discrimination issue, since a formal arrest is not the beginning of the defendant's interaction with the system. A number of important (and perhaps discriminatory) decisions have already been made. In fact, some have argued that these prearrest decisions hold the most potential for discrimination, since they occur in one of the least visible phases of the justice system (Green, 1964). It is well known that the police exercise considerable discretion in enforcing the law. Officers may ignore certain offenses because of manpower limitations, public pressure, or simple preference. Police administrators rarely have formal arrest criteria, but usually rely on the individual officer's judgment. Given this latitude in decisionmaking, there is great potential for discrimination. Unfortunately, decisions reached in these early phases of the justice process go unrecorded, and researchers are unable to determine the extent to which members of racial minority groups are treated more harshly because of their race.

An equally important omission in previous research has been the failure to study the handling of minorities *after* sentencing. The sentencing decision is certainly not the end of the defendant's interaction with the system. For those sentenced to prison, it is just the beginning of many interactions that result in important decisions. Again, much of this decisionmaking goes unrecorded and is thus unreviewable. For example, a correctional officer frequently witnesses behavior that could qualify as a prison disciplinary infraction. Whether he chooses to record it formally or ignore it is almost totally discretionary. If he chooses to record it, he also has great latitude in meting out punishment. The range of punishments is wide: solitary confinement, loss of work assignment or other privileges, or time added to the sentence. These decisions profoundly affect the conditions under which an inmate serves his sentence, and even the length of time he will serve.

This research project is designed to correct for both poor methodology and the lack of a system-wide approach. The data we will analyze bear on decisionmaking from crime commission through release from custody.

Our study uses the two sources of data described in the Introduction: California's Offender-Based Transaction Statistics (OBTS) for 1980, and the Rand Inmate Survey (RIS).[4] We use the Inmate Survey

---

[4]The Rand Inmate Survey was originally funded by the National Institute of Justice to serve the needs of two research projects. The first project examined the characteristics of career criminals, and the second determined whether career criminals posed

to examine the prearrest and postconviction process and the OBTS for the process from formal arrest through final disposition. We briefly describe these data bases below.

THE OFFENDER-BASED TRANSACTION STATISTICS (OBTS)

The OBTS is a computerized information system maintained by the Bureau of Criminal Statistics (BCS). It tracks an offender from the point of entry into the criminal justice system to the point of exit. (The unit of analysis is the case, not the individual. A single individual may be involved in more than one case.) The purpose is to collect statistical information on how the California criminal justice system deals with persons arrested on felony charges. The data reflect dispositions that occurred in a given year as a result of an adult felony arrest made in that year or in previous years.[5]

Once an offender enters the system, a number of social and legal variables are recorded. Descriptive information includes sex, race, age, prior record, criminal status, and the offense for which he was originally arrested (original charge). Prior record is a measure of previous exposure to the criminal justice system referring not only to the number but also to the seriousness of prior commitments. The measure ranges from 0 to 9, with 0 designating lack of previous arrests or convictions and 9 designating three or more prior prison commitments. Intermediate categories represent various combinations of arrests and sentences of increasing seriousness.

Criminal status refers to whether or not an offender was under some type of supervision (and the nature of that supervision) at the time of his arrest. Various possibilities include parole from the California Department of Corrections or the California Youth Authority, probation, and the like.

Once the offender begins to be formally processed by the system, information regarding each transaction is recorded. The system tracks the offender until his case is disposed of in either the lower or Superior Court. Section III describes the information recorded about disposition.

---

particular problems once incarcerated. The results from the analysis of these two previous projects are contained in Chaiken and Chaiken (1982), Greenwood (1982), Petersilia and Honig (1980), and Petersilia (1982).

[5]This is different from arrest data. Arrest data are based upon the year in which the arrest took place. OBTS data are based upon the year of disposition, regardless of when the felony arrest occurred, and may be reported a year or more after the arrest was made.

OBTS information is forwarded by law enforcement, prosecutor, and court agencies in all 58 California counties. BCS estimates that it receives reports on no more than 70 percent of adult felony arrests that receive final dispositions during a calendar year. In spite of this underreporting, it is felt that the reports adequately describe the "statewide" processing of these arrestees (California Bureau of Criminal Statistics, 1980). The analysis in this report uses OBTS data for 1980.

THE RAND INMATE SURVEY (RIS)

Sample Selection

In 1978, Rand administered a questionnaire to selected prison inmates in California, Michigan, and Texas. These states were chosen for the Inmate Survey because they have large prison systems, they house 22 percent of all persons serving time in a state prison (Bureau of Justice Statistics, 1982), and they maintain computerized prison records, which facilitated the selection of the sample.

We identified three or four prisons in each state that provided an adequate cross-section of the male prison population. The prisons included all custody levels within each prison system. The prisons from which inmates were sampled include:

California: California Correctional Institution (Tehachapi)
Correctional Training Facility (Soledad)
Deuel Vocational Institution (Tracy)
San Quentin Penitentiary (San Rafael)

Michigan: Ionia Reformatory (Ionia)
Michigan Training Unit (Ionia)
State Prison of Southern Michigan (Jackson)

Texas: Ellis Unit (Huntsville)
Coffield Unit (Tennessee Colony)
Ferguson Unit (Midway)
Wynne Unit (Huntsville)

In each state, our final inmate sample was representative of the statewide intake of male prisoners.[6] Table 2.1 compares the

---

[6]To approximate an "incoming cohort" in each state, it was not possible merely to select a random sample of current inmates. Such a sample, where each inmate serving

distribution of four characteristics—race, age, conviction offense, and prior prison commitments—for the statewide prison population and the Rand samples. There are no statistically significant differences except in two instances: For California, the Rand sample contains a larger proportion of whites; and for Texas, the Rand sample is somewhat older ($\chi^2 < .05$).

Survey Administration

The RIS questionnaire contained 174 questions, some multiparted. It required one to two hours to complete. There were numerous skip patterns, and the majority of respondents were not required to answer all the questions. The survey elicited information about the inmate's crimes, arrests, crime motivations, drug and alcohol use, prior criminal record, and prison experiences.

The survey was not anonymous. It included only those inmates who signed an agreement indicating their understanding and their willingness to participate. Usually, the questionnaire was administered to groups ranging from only a few inmates to as many as 40 or 50 (20 was typical). Each inmate who completed the questionnaire received $5 as compensation.[7]

To complement the questionnaires, we compiled official records data from hardcopy corrections files on the participating inmates. We coded data relating to intake recommendations, prior criminal records, current prison infractions, and demographics. The official

---

a prison term has an equal likelihood of being selected, would overrepresent prisoners serving long sentences and underrepresent prisoners with very short sentences, because those with long sentences are more likely to still be in prison. To compensate for this bias, we gave each current inmate a weight equal to the reciprocal of the expected length of his current term as a sample selection factor. These lists were sent to each institution so that the survey sessions could be scheduled; the institutions then notified these inmates about the sessions. Separate inmate notification was given by the Rand staff as well. To avoid bias in the sample, we devised a "replacement" procedure. For each inmate selected for the sample, another inmate of similar race, age, and county of commitment was also selected as his "replacement." When the initially selected sample member did not appear at the survey sessions, or chose not to participate, his replacement was sought.

[7]Because certain inmates within segregated custody were regarded by prison officials as posing security risks if assembled into a group, for the survey, the questionnaire was administered to them individually within their segregated custody. Completed questionnaires were obtained from nearly all selected inmates having this status. Also, some inmates could not read English; this was especially true of Spanish-speaking inmates in California. The survey instrument was translated into Spanish for those persons.

Table 2.1

COMPARISON OF INMATE CHARACTERISTICS BETWEEN STATEWIDE PRISON POPULATION AND RAND SAMPLES
(In percent)

Characteristic	California Statewide Prison Population[a]	California Rand Sample	Michigan Statewide Prison Population	Michigan Rand Sample	Texas Statewide Prison Population	Texas Rand Sample
Race						
White	36	44	30	32	40	38
Hispanic	23	20	2	3	10	10
Black	39	36	68	65	50	52
Other	2	0	0	0	0	0
Age[b]						
23 or less	25	27	39	43	52	36
24-30	49	50	31	33	23	37
31 or more	26	23	30	24	25	27
Conviction offense[c]						
Homicide	8	11	8	10	5	6
Robbery	35	37	16	21	18	20
Assault	6	8	14	15	5	6
Burglary	23	16	24	15	36	39
Theft/forgery	9	9	6	12	8	10
Rape	3	5	9	10	3	3
Drugs	10	7	6	7	10	9
Other	6	6	17	10	16	7
Prior prison commitment(s)						
No	63	67	60	60	67	64
Yes	37	33	40	40	33	36

[a]As approximated by the initially selected sample.
[b]At time of completing the questionnaire.
[c]Most serious of conviction offenses.

record data served both in the analysis and in the verification of some of the survey information.

Survey Response Rates

Usable questionnaires were obtained from a total of 1380 prisoners, including those who were replacements for initially selected inmates who failed to appear. The response rate was 73 percent, with component rates in the percentages as shown in Table 2.2.

Table 2.2

INMATE SURVEY RESPONSE RATES

(In percent)

State	Completed Survey	Usable[a] Survey Completed	Usable Survey Paired with Official Record
California	61	57 (n=357)	55 (n=342)
Michigan	64	62 (n=422)	51 (n=346)
Texas	92	82 (n=601)	72 (n=527)
Combined	73	69 (n=1380)	60 (n=1214)

[a]Usable surveys were those decipherable. In Texas, a large number of surveys completed by the "replacement" sample were deleted because the primary respondents showed up to complete the survey in a later session (after the replacements had already been called). Inclusion of these replacements would have distorted the characteristics of the original sample.

We believe that the disparities in response rates among states primarily reflect differences in control and administration of the various institutions. The major source of nonresponse was failure to appear at the survey sessions. We attribute these absences mainly to inadequate notification. Once they appeared at a survey session (approximately 75 percent of those notified), only about 10 percent refused to complete the survey.

Our results derive from two samples: the "Usable Survey Completed" and the "Usable Survey Paired with Official Record." For analyzing crime commission rates and arrest probabilities, we use the sample of all usable questionnaires (n = 1380). However, for analyzing sentence length, prison treatment, and work programs, we could use only questionnaires that were matched with official records (n = 1214). Table 2.3 shows the final sample size by state and race.

Accuracy of the Responses

The structure of the survey and associated data collection efforts enabled us to explore the integrity of the inmate responses in a num-

Table 2.3

FINAL SAMPLE SIZE, BY STATE AND RACE

Race	California	Michigan	Texas	Total
	Survey Sample[a]			
White	159 (44%)	135 (32%)	227 (38%)	521 (38%)
Black	130 (36%)	276 (65%)	312 (52%)	718 (52%)
Hispanic	68 (20%)	11 (3%)	62 (10%)	141 (10%)
Total	357	422	601	1380
	Survey Plus Official Records[b]			
White	152 (44%)	113 (33%)	193 (37%)	461 (38%)
Black	126 (37%)	223 (64%)	277 (53%)	624 (51%)
Hispanic	64 (19%)	10 (3%)	56 (11%)	130 (11%)
Total	342	346	526	1214

[a]Used for analyzing offense rates, arrest probabilities, weapon use, and crime motivation.

[b]Used when information from the official record was merged with the Inmate Survey (i.e., the analysis of prior violence and work program participation and sentence length served).

ber of ways. The survey included pairs of questions, widely separated, that asked for essentially the same information about crimes the respondents had committed and about other topics. This made it possible to check for internal quality (inconsistency, omission, and confusion). Over 83 percent of the respondents filled out the questionnaire very accurately, completely, and consistently. Over 95 percent were able to follow the fairly complex skip patterns in the survey booklet and to fill out the calendar that showed the time period being studied. The official records showed that 85 percent of the prisoners filled out their calendars correctly to the month (Chaiken and Chaiken, 1982).

Access to official records enabled an external check of the self-reports' validity. Although the external comparison of the validity of the responses did not yield as favorable results as the check of their internal reliability, approximately 60 percent of the prisoners had an external error rate of less than 20 percent. (Nearly half had two or fewer disparities out of the 14 categories checked, less than 7 percent had between six and nine disparities, and none had more than nine.) However, for most disparities, the records' validity and completeness are as suspect as the respondent's veracity: Prisoners' records are often missing or incomplete—through no fault of theirs.[8] An analysis of the accuracy of the inmate self-reports showed that estimates of the numbers of arrests and convictions obtained from self-reports were unbiased or, in a few instances, higher than the official record estimate (Marquis and Ebener, 1981).

Chaiken and Chaiken (1982) analyzed two samples of inmates. The first involved all respondents, and the second excluded the 42 percent whose truthfulness they had even the slightest reason to doubt (it excluded even the prisoners with missing or incomplete official records). Their purpose was to determine whether such exclusion would affect the estimates of the overall crime commission rates. They found that the estimates were not significantly or consistently affected when the suspect group was included.

Chaiken and Chaiken also compared several inmate characteristics with the indicators of the quality of the self-report data. One might suspect that some types of people would be less truthful in self-reports than others. With minor exceptions, such characteristics as conviction crime, self-image, activity in fraud or "illegal cons," and sociodemographic characteristics were unrelated to the quality and validity of the individuals' response.

We were particularly interested in whether the responses of minority inmates were less valid and reliable than those from nonminorities. Minority persons accounted for a majority of the survey administration staff. We believe that minority representation on the Rand staff was important for gaining the trust of the respondents. (Survey administrators also had prior criminal justice experience.)

Mexican-Americans proved to have no better or worse external validity or internal quality than did other respondents. Black respondents were no better or worse than other respondents on external validity, but had worse internal quality, in particular with regard to confusion and inconsistency, but not to omissions (Chaiken and Chaiken, 1982).

In sum, we found the self-reports data sufficiently valid and reliable to serve as a credible basis for our study of racial disparities.

---

[8]Juvenile records suffer notably in this regard. In nearly all cases of disparity between the self-reports and juvenile records, the respondent admitted to juvenile crimes or incarceration, but the record showed none (Chaiken and Chaiken, 1982).

III.   RACIAL DIFFERENCES IN CASE PROCESSING: ARREST THROUGH SENTENCING

Official records tell a limited story about the people involved in the criminal justice process and the legal and extralegal factors that may affect their treatment. As Sec. II indicated, one drawback is lack of information on the pre-arrest and post-sentencing stages. But even for those stages usually represented in official data, the information routinely collected is scant. Most records maintained by criminal justice agencies contain little more information about the offender than his age, race, prior record, and offense (usually one of a broad offense grouping). Nevertheless, official records provide the objective base for beginning a study of possible discrimination.

The OBTS data allowed us to examine the felony disposition process in California for any indications that minorities are treated differently at key decision points. Specifically, this section will examine whether minorities have a greater probability of (1) having their case officially filed, once arrested; (2) being convicted, once charges are filed; (3) receiving a prison sentence, once convicted; and (4) serving a longer prison sentence after conviction. To investigate the last point, we used the wider data base provided by the RIS.

THE FELONY DISPOSITION PROCESS AT WORK

Each year more than 1.5 million adults in the United States enter the felony disposition process. This process, beginning with arrest and ending with either the dropping of charges or sentencing, is the heart of the criminal justice system. It is commonly referred to as a funnel or sieve because a great many persons enter the process but very few remain at the end. Approximately 30 percent of the arrestees are dismissed before the preliminary hearing; less than half of those who go to court are convicted; and less than 5 percent of those convicted are sentenced to prison (Greenwood, 1982).

The California process resembles that of other states in all but a few aspects. Prosecution of a felony charge usually begins with a police arrest, with or without a warrant. The police make arrests without warrants, "on-view" arrests, based on probable cause—that is, subjective belief that a felony has been committed by a specific person. To

14

make probable cause credible, there must be a set of facts that would justify that belief in a reasonable person. Arrests made with warrants differ in that the facts of the case are evaluated as they would be for filing a charge.[1] Consequently, evidence for warrant arrests is generally stronger.

Within a set time after arrest (usually 48 to 96 hours), the police must obtain a formal complaint from the District Attorney or release the defendant. Under California law, the law enforcement agency that makes the arrest may release the person from custody if it is "satisfied that there are insufficient grounds for making a criminal complaint against the person arrested."[2] If the police decide to seek a complaint, they present the case information to a deputy in the District Attorney's office for screening. The deputy reviews the police reports and the defendant's prior record, and may talk to the officer about the case. He may then file a felony complaint, file a misdemeanor complaint, suggest that the police investigate further, or reject the case. The District Attorney files a felony charge if:

- There is legally sufficient, admissible evidence of the *corpus delicti* of the crime,
- There is legally sufficient, admissible evidence of the identity of the perpetrator of the crime,
- The prosecutor believes that the evidence shows the guilt of the accused,
- The evidence is so convincing that it would warrant conviction by an objective fact-finder.

It is apparent that the charging standard that underlies a complaint is much higher than the probable-cause standard that supports an arrest. The complaint filing function is one of the most sensitive and important because it moves a case onto one of two largely irreversible tracks. If the complaint is rejected and the police agree, it is lost from the system without much chance for review. Once it is filed, the system presses on with it.

If a decision is made to file, the defendant is arraigned in Municipal Court, where he is informed of the charges. At this hearing, the defendant will usually apply for bail or for release on his own recognizance. He then either meets the release conditions (for example, posting bond) or is committed to pretrial detention (jail).

Although he is not required to plead at this time, and it is unusual for him to do so, he can enter a plea. If he pleads not guilty, a date is

---

[1] Indeed, in many cases, a warrant is issued by a court based on a complaint filed by the District Attorney.
[2] Penal Code 849(b)(1).

set, usually one week later, for a preliminary hearing at which the District Attorney presents evidence, either to the magistrate or the Grand Jury, that the defendant committed the felony. That evidence must be sufficient to establish a prima facie case—that is, sufficient to convict the defendant if it is unchallenged by the defense.

The end result of the preliminary hearing is either that the defendant is bound over to the Superior Court, the charge is reduced to a misdemeanor, or the felony charges are simply dropped. Only Superior Court judges can sentence upon felony cases. Thus, if the court decides that the District Attorney has a valid felony case, it binds the defendant over to Superior Court. However, a felony case can also reach the Superior Court if the defendant pleads guilty in Municipal Court. In such cases, the defendant is "certified" to the Superior Court for trial and sentence. Under California law (Penal Code 17(b)), many felony charges can be handled as either felonies or misdemeanors. These so-called "wobblers" result in a number of cases that were originally charged as felonies being processed in the lower courts as misdemeanors and never reaching the Superior Court.

After a defendant is certified to the Superior Court, he is formally arraigned, defense counsel is appointed for him if he is indigent, and he must enter a plea. At some point between arraignment and trial, most defendants decide to plead guilty—usually the result of plea bargaining between the prosecutor and the defense. Plea bargaining usually results in less severe sentencing, reduction of charges, or both.

If plea bargaining fails, the case proceeds to trial, and the defendant is either convicted or acquitted of each of the charges. If convicted, the court imposes sentence. The sentencing decision includes imposing both the nature of the sentence (e.g., fine, jail, probation, prison) and its length.

In passing sentence, a judge usually follows the recommendation contained in a presentence investigation report (PSR) prepared by the Probation Officer. These reports differ in format, but a primary objective is to provide information for assessing the defendant's potentiality for rehabilitation or recidivism. Currently, many states are shortening PSRs, often employing objective checklists of recidivism indicators derived from actuarial tables. However, the traditional PSR in most states has been a lengthy, quasi-biographical document describing the defendant's background, history, and personal and socioeconomic characteristics. Although these are much more inclusive and impressionistic than simple checklists, evidence indicates that sentencing recommendations are based on only a few pieces of information (e.g., prior record, employment status, social stability, family history). PSRs are very influential documents: In over 80 percent of cases, judges follow their recommendations in passing sentence (Carter, 1978). Not only that, the PSR provides a great deal of the material used by prison and parole boards to make parole decisions.

PRIOR RESEARCH

Previous research has a great deal to say about how minorities are treated as they pass through this system, but the findings on discrimination are highly contradictory. Some studies have found harsher treatment accorded to minorities, others have found no differences, and still others have found that minorities are treated more leniently. Despite these contradictions, there is general agreement in the literature about the factors that increase the likelihood of conviction and the severity of sentences, regardless of race:

- Severity of offense
- Degree of violence involved
- Multiple charges
- Seriousness of initial charge
- Seriousness of prior criminal record
- Possession of weapons
- Failure to make bail
- Length of pretrial detention
- Type of attorney (privately paid lawyer, publicly appointed lawyer, or public defender)[3]

In a recent review of discrimination studies for a National Academy of Science panel on sentencing, Garber et al. conclude:

> Virtually all the studies suggest that three factors are of particular importance in the processing of cases through the CJS: seriousness of the offense, quality of the evidence, and the prior record of the defendant. These factors are measured in various ways. . . . Seriousness of the offense appears to be particularly relevant in the decision to prosecute, the charge, the size of bail, and in sentence (given conviction). It also appears to be an important factor affecting the defendant's choice of attorney. . . . The quality of the evidence appears to play an important role in the decision to prosecute, the choice of plea, and trial conviction. . . . Prior record plays an important role in the decision to prosecute, the size of the bail, sentencing, and (to some degree) in conviction (1982, p. 6).

---

[3]See Bernstein et al. (1977); Clarke (1982); Feeley (1979). Other researchers have identified less generally recognized factors. For example, Meyers' (1980) research on conviction decisions found that when victim and defendant were strangers or when victims were of high employment status or highly educated, there was greater likelihood of conviction.

Garber et al. further observe that other legal and quasi-legal factors are also important at some stages. Making bail consistently appears to affect case disposition. It presumably operates through the conviction process by affecting the defendant's ability to put together a successful defense. In some studies, the quality of legal representation and the type of plea also seem to be influential.

Despite general agreement on these factors, studies of possible discrimination in case disposition have failed to reach consensus on any other point. Ever since the 1960s, researchers have found some evidence for discrimination in sentencing for certain kinds of crime, and in particular points of the criminal justice process. But others find no consistent discrimination. In an evaluation of earlier research, Hindelang (1969) suggests that divergent findings in the literature published prior to 1966 might be explained by the fact that (1) studies finding racial discrimination used data from Southern states, (2) studies finding discrimination used data about ten years older than those in studies finding no race discrimination, and (3) studies finding no discrimination were more careful in controlling for nonracial variables. It may also be true that two studies that reach different conclusions on discrimination might both be correct. Discrimination is not uniform across judges' jurisdictions, parts of the system, or time periods. However, poor methodology appears to account for most of the inconclusiveness found in early work.

Although recent studies are generally more methodologically rigorous, use more recent data, and include a wider variety of offenses than the earlier studies did, their findings are still contradictory.[4] Even when studies have rigorously controlled for many of the legal and quasi-legal factors noted above, they have still disagreed about how fairly the felony disposition system treats minorities. Lizotte's (1978) data on Chicago courts show "gross discrimination" on the basis of race and occupation. In that study, all other things being equal, blacks of low socioeconomic status (SES) received prison sentences at least eight months longer than whites who had higher SES.

These findings are consistent with a recent study by Zalman et al. (1979). Using Michigan data, they found statistically significant differences in the sentence type (in/out) and sentence length for defendants charged with sex crimes. Using regression equations, they found that 64 percent of whites can be expected to be incarcerated for a sex crime conviction, while 78 percent of nonwhites will be incar-

---

[4]For example, several studies find little or no effect of race on sentencing: Burke and Turk (1975); Chiricos and Waldo (1975); Bernstein, Kelly, and Doyle (1977); Perry (1977); Cohen and Kluegel (1978); McCarthy (1979); and Clarke and Koch (1977). Several others *do* find a relationship: Arnold (1971); Chiricos, Jackson, and Waldo (1972); Hagan (1975); Swigert and Farrell (1977); Lizotte (1978); and Zalman et al. (1979).

cerated. White defendants convicted of sex crimes were sentenced to a mean term of 46 months, while nonwhites averaged 91 months. With respect to other crime types, they found that nonwhites receive harsher sentences for homicide, assault, robbery, burglary, and larceny. Nonwhites had anywhere from 0.07 to 0.15 higher probability of being incarcerated for these crimes than whites.

The analysis of sentence length by Zalman et al. found fewer instances of racial disparity, although there were statistically significant differences in the crimes of sex, drug, burglary, and larceny. In all four instances, nonwhites were treated more harshly than whites (Zalman et al., 1979, p. 234). They conclude:

> Taken together, the results of an analysis of the IN/OUT and LENGTH decisions indicate that there is evidence of very distinct differences in the treatment of whites and nonwhites. Furthermore, in all cases in which the differences are statistically significant, nonwhites are being treated more severely.

In contrast, a study of sentencing in New Jersey concluded that:

> Racially different but otherwise similar offenders convicted of similar offenses receive similar sentences. That is, *when statistically accounting for the effect of key factors relating to the nature of the offender and offense*, the data do not support the contention that minority race offenders receive more severe sentences than similar white offenders (McCarthy et al., 1979).

This agrees with the Clarke and Koch (1977) finding that in burglary and larceny sentences in Charlotte, North Carolina, offense, criminal history, and promptness of apprehension have predictive associations with prison sentences, but there is "no evidence that the defendant's age, race, or employment status had an important relationship to prison outcome."

Nevertheless, the only stage at which extralegal factors such as age, race, and SES have *not* been found to play a role, in one study or another, is the conviction stage (although only La Free (1980a, 1980b) studies convictions directly). Moreover, several studies emphasize the cumulative role of extralegal factors. By the time black and lower-status defendants reach the sentencing stage, they are claimed to be at a considerable disadvantage. They appear to face more serious charges, be more often induced to plead guilty, be less able to make bail and thus organize a successful defense, and have restricted access to good legal representation. All of these factors are believed to affect sentence and case disposition generally. Swigert and Farrell (1977) also note that discrimination can start a vicious cycle, contributing to the creation and growth of a criminal record that in turn leads to harsher treatment in subsequent encounters with the criminal justice system.

ADULT FELONY PROSECUTION IN CALIFORNIA

The OBTS for 1980 provided the official data for our study of racial differences in case processing. The OBTS traces cases in which adults were arrested for *felony* offenses from the point of arrest through final disposition. The unit of analysis is a case, not a defendant. It is common for a defendant to be involved in multiple cases. The OBTS contains information on the following case elements:[5]

- Race, sex
- Prior criminal record (e.g., none, minor, major)
- Criminal status (e.g., parole, probation)
- Type of arrest charge
- Point of disposition
- Type of proceedings
- Type of disposition
- Type of sentence

As this list indicates, the OBTS does not provide information on some of the factors just described that could affect case processing. For example, it does not contain information related to bail or type of attorney.[6] It did not allow us to go behind the initial charging decision to explore how often intentional overcharging occurs. Nor did it permit us to assess the quality of evidence in the case, the defendant's SES or his demeanor, and other factors related to case processing. Thus, the OBTS has limitations for our purposes.

Nevertheless, the data were sufficient to raise some general questions about racial differences in case processing and allow us to determine whether defendants of different races who were charged with similar crimes and had similar records were treated differently. The data permitted us to examine "system fallout" for California felony arrestees as a whole and to compare treatment of whites, blacks, and Hispanics at various key points in the felony disposition system. However, overall, these comparisons do not control simultaneously for crime type, prior record, age, or criminal status. Without those con-

---

[5]In addition to the elements listed, the OBTS also contains data on sentence length. However, we preferred to use the RIS for this analysis because it represents sentencing practices in several states.

[6]OBTS stopped collecting "type of attorney" information in 1978.

trols, it is impossible to assess the validity of apparent racial differences in sentencing. To overcome that problem, we conducted a more detailed analysis of case processing for robbery arrestees in Los Angeles County, using multiple regression techniques.

Case Disposition for All Felony Arrestees in 1980

Figure 3.1 shows the fallout that occurs at the eight stages between arrest and sentencing disposition. A final disposition can occur at the law enforcement, prosecution, lower court, or Superior Court level. The descending curve describes the fallout. For example, 10.6 percent of arrestees were released by the police, thus lowering the curve that much. The remaining 89.4 percent represent the proportion of the cases in the system still awaiting disposition, and so forth. In 1980, 55.8 percent of the arrestees in these cases were convicted, and 6.1 percent were sentenced to state institutions, which include prison, Youth Authority, California Rehabilitation Center, and state hospitals. The remainder (44.2 percent) were not convicted.

Figure 3.2 presents the system fallout percentages separately for the three races. The spaces between the curves depict differences in

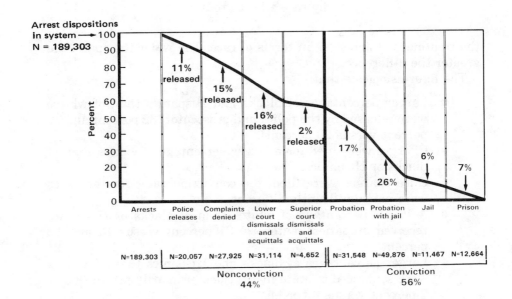

Fig. 3.1—Dispositions of adult felony arrests, 1980
system fallout

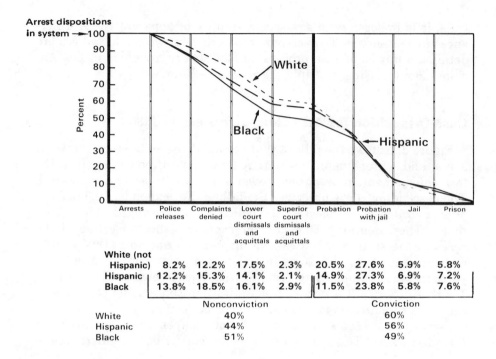

	Arrests	Police releases	Complaints denied	Lower court dismissals and acquittals	Superior court dismissals and acquittals	Probation	Probation with jail	Jail	Prison
White (not Hispanic)	8.2%	12.2%	17.5%	2.3%	20.5%	27.6%	5.9%	5.8%	
Hispanic	12.2%	15.3%	14.1%	2.1%	14.9%	27.3%	6.9%	7.2%	
Black	13.8%	18.5%	16.1%	2.9%	11.5%	23.8%	5.8%	7.6%	

	Nonconviction	Conviction
White	40%	60%
Hispanic	44%	56%
Black	51%	49%

Fig. 3.2—Dispositions of adult felony arrests, 1980,
by race/ethnic group

the treatment of arrestees in terms of race. The wider the space, the greater the difference.

The figure suggests that:

- Larger percentages of blacks and Hispanics than of whites were released by the police and prosecutor (32 percent and 27 percent versus 20 percent),
- Charges were filed for a larger percentage of whites than of blacks or Hispanics,
- Once charges were filed, the conviction rates for the races were not significantly different,
- A larger percentage of whites than of blacks or Hispanics received probation sentences (21 percent versus 15 and 12 percent),
- Larger percentages of blacks and Hispanics than of whites were sentenced to state institutions, primarily prison (8 and 7 percent versus 6 percent).

The relative positions of the curves suggest that whites are treated more severely than blacks and Hispanics at the beginning of the felony disposition process but more leniently at the end. When we examine treatment of the races at key decision points in that process, this suggestion is confirmed.

Treatment of Races at Key Points in the System

At Arrest. Police make some arrests with warrants and some "on view." In both cases, they operate on probable cause. However, an arrest made with a warrant has already been screened by the District Attorney, using the criteria for filing a complaint. Consequently, warrant arrests are usually made on stronger evidence than on-view arrests are.

The OBTS data show that in the original population of arrests for 1980, proportionately more blacks and Hispanics were arrested on view (Table 3.1). This finding occurs when we combine all felonies or examine selected types. Throughout this section we examine dispositions for homicide, rape, robbery, burglary, as well as all felonies combined.

Release or Filing. At this point, the suspect may be released by either the law enforcement agency that made the arrest or by the prosecutor. Either one may decide that the evidence in the case will not support a complaint or that there is some obstruction to filing. The prosecutor may also reduce the felony arrest to a misdemeanor complaint. Table 3.2 indicates what happened at this point for all 1980 felony arrests and for our four selected crimes.

Table 3.1

PERCENTAGES OF ARRESTEES ARRESTED "ON VIEW"

Arrest Charge	Arrestee's Race		
	White	Black	Hispanic
Homicide	94	96	96
Rape	98	98	98
Robbery	95	99	99
Burglary	96	99	99
Other felonies	90	93	93
All felonies combined	91	94	94

Table 3.2

POLICE/PROSECUTOR ACTIONS
(Percent of Those Reaching That Stage)

	Arrestee's Race		
Action	White	Black	Hispanic
Released by police			
Homicide	21	19	21
Rape	19	19	31
Robbery	27	29	24
Burlary	18	22	18
All felonies combined	9	13	12
Prosecutor denies complaint			
Homicide	8	13	14
Rape	22	35	27
Robbery	15	18	20
Burglary	10	11	14
All felonies combined	13	18	16
Prosecutor files misdemeanor charges			
Homicide	6	6	8
Rape	18	7	11
Robbery	20	17	21
Burglary	46	41	43
All felonies combined	41	33	37
Prosecutor files felony charges			
Homicide	65	61	56
Rape	41	38	32
Robbery	39	36	34
Burglary	26	22	24
All felonies combined	38	35	35

There is an expected and inevitable decrease in cases from felony arrests to criminal charges filed. Two agencies are involved in the early release of the defendants: the police and the prosecutor. The data permit a rough breakdown of the reasons for release. Table 3.3 combines all felony offense types; similar trends were obtained for each of the offense types.

Table 3.3

REASONS FOR RELEASE, FOR ALL FELONIES COMBINED
(Percent of Those Released at That Stage)

	Arrestee's Race		
Agency and Reason	White	Black	Hispanic
Police release			
Insufficient evidence	4	6	6
Exonerated	1	1	1
Victim refused to prosecute	2	3	2
Other	2	3	3
Prosecutor denies complaint			
Lack of corpus	3	3	3
Lack of probable cause	6	7	6
Interest of justice	1	1	1
Victim refuses to prosecute	1	2	2
Witness unavailable	0	1	1
Illegal search	1	1	0
Other	1	3	3

If we combine the reasons for police and prosecutor release, we see that insufficient evidence accounted for approximately 95 percent of those released. This disproportion reflects the basic difference between the grounds for on-view arrests and the grounds for filing charges. Consider a typical case: The robbery victim gives police a description of the robbers and the car they are driving. Shortly thereafter, the police stop and arrest the occupants of a car, both the car and its occupants matching the description. This arrest on probable cause may produce direct or circumstantial evidence that meets the necessary beyond-a-reasonable-doubt standard of proof to support a robbery complaint, but it may not. If no physical evidence linked to the robbery turns up and the victim cannot identify the arrested persons in a line-up, no charge will be filed.

The data show racial disproportion in filing and release for on-view arrests. Of arrested whites, 21.2 percent were not charged, as opposed to 31.5 percent for blacks and 28.0 percent for Hispanics. These data suggest that blacks and Hispanics in California are more likely than whites to be arrested under circumstances that provide insufficient evidence to support criminal charges. We discuss the possible implications of this phenomenon later.

Lower Court Actions. Following a felony charge, the defendant appears for a hearing in Municipal Court. After the District Attorney presents evidence to the magistrate or Grand Jury, the case may be dismissed, bound over to Superior Court as a felony, or tried in the lower court as a misdemeanor under Sec. 17(b) of the Penal Code. We found that once felony charges are filed, defendants of all races have roughly the same chance of being *prosecuted* on felony charges.

Adjudication. When defendants are prosecuted on a felony charge, chances of conviction are also fairly even for whites, blacks, and Hispanics. However, some defendants are acquitted, some convictions are for misdemeanor offenses only, and, again, some cases are dismissed. Plea bargaining strongly affects case disposition, and most cases reach disposition by plea. Cases go to trial (by jury or judge) only if a satisfactory plea bargain cannot be reached. Only 7 percent of the white defendants were tried by a jury, but 12 percent of the blacks and 11 percent of the Hispanics were. Table 3.4 shows the result of the adjudication of felony cases in 1980. These figures show that white defendants had a slightly higher conviction rate than minorities. However, that may be related to the fact that they also engaged more in plea bargaining, which virtually guarantees conviction. Similar trends were obtained for each of the separate crime types as well.

Sentencing. In the California system, the number of possible sentences is amazing. In addition to state prison, there are state-level dispositions involving custody in other state institutions; the California Youth Authority (CYA); the California Rehabilitation Center (CRC) for narcotic addicts; facilities for Mentally Disordered Sex Offenders (MDSO); and mental health facilities for persons found Not Guilty by Reason of Insanity (NGI). At the local level, there is the possibility of county jail either as a condition of probation or as a direct sentence, and, finally, there is the possibility of a disposition without a requirement of state or local custody.[7]

---

[7]There were 23 persons sentenced to death in 1980: 10 whites, 4 Hispanics, 8 blacks, 1 other.

Table 3.4

FINAL CASE OUTCOMES FOR ALL FELONIES COMBINED,
LOS ANGELES COUNTY SUPERIOR COURT, 1980
(Percent of All Cases)

Outcome	Arrestee's Race		
	White	Black	Hispanic
Felony charge in Superior Court	23	24	22
Conviction	20	20	19
Conviction rate	87	83	86
Percent of convictions by plea	92	85	87

There is an apparent racial disproportion in the prison commitment rate. Hispanics and blacks were more likely to be sentenced to prison after a felony conviction than whites. (See Table 3.5.)

To this point, the analysis has concentrated on the processing of felonies as felonies. The OBTS data showed that almost half of the felony arrests were processed as misdemeanors. Some cases were processed as misdemeanors based on the original charge decision by the District Attorney, and others were handled in the Municipal Court, although charged originally as felonies, through the "wobbler" mechanism of Penal Code 17(b). The misdemeanor results resemble those for felonies. Here again, the white suspect was more likely to be charged with a misdemeanor, but had about an equal chance of conviction. Black and Hispanic defendants were more likely than whites to be sentenced to county jail upon conviction.

By analyzing the outcomes at each decision point, we have fleshed out the picture of racial differences implied by Fig. 3.2. Once arrested, minorities evidently are more likely than white suspects to be released. However, once convicted of misdemeanors, minorities are more likely than whites to go to jail instead of getting probation. And once convicted of felonies, they are more likely to receive prison sentences. Nevertheless, these findings do not necessarily imply discrimination at the sentencing stage.

Table 3.5

SUPERIOR COURT SENTENCES BY RACE, LOS ANGELES COUNTY, 1980

(Percent of Those Arrested)

Sentence and Arrest Offense	Defendant's Race		
	White	Black	Hispanic
Probation (with or without jail)			
Homicide	29	33	51
Rape	47	33	51
Robbery	61	54	60
Burglary	75	68	70
All felonies combined	71	67	65
State-level incarceration[a]			
Homicide	66	74	75
Rape	45	64	40
Robbery	37	45	38
Burglary	13	16	14
All felonies combined	28	33	35

[a]Includes prison, California Youth Authority, California Rehabilitation Center, and state hospitals.

These aggregate findings treat all felonies as if they were the same. If minority defendants had more serious prior records, we would expect them to be treated more severely by the criminal justice system. We know from the data that minorities in the 1980 OBTS did have more serious prior records and that more of them were on conditional status, that is, on probation or parole (California Department of Justice, 1980). After controlling for these and other factors using multiple regression techniques, we found that the racial differences in post-arrest and sentencing treatment still held.

Processing of Robbery Arrestees in Los Angeles County

To analyze the processing of robbery arrestees, we used defendants who were charged with robbery in Los Angeles County in 1980 (n = 6652, or about 10 percent of all the Los Angeles cases on the OBTS tape). We limited the analysis to a single county and a single crime type because of the expense in processing so large a data base as this one, and because previous research using the OBTS file had shown significant differences in the processing of defendants from different counties and arrested on different charges (Pope, 1975b). To study racial differences, we wanted a population that was homogeneous with respect to county and arrest charge. The regression analysis was designed to test for racial differences in the probability of going to prison if convicted.

Our Los Angeles results are consistent with the statewide data. White suspects in Los Angeles County were more likely than minorities to be officially charged following a robbery arrest. Black arrestees were more likely to have their cases dismissed either by the police or prosecutor. Minority defendants were less likely to settle their cases through plea bargaining. Also, a greater proportion of minority arrestees were arrested "on view."

The conviction rates were similar across the races. Also, there were no statistically significant differences in the type of robbery that persons of the different races were convicted of, e.g., attempted robbery, robbery, or assault to rob.

To determine whether minorities were sentenced to prison more frequently, we selected persons from the arrest sample who were convicted in the Superior Court (n = 2193). The sentences they received for some offense (as a result of a robbery arrest) were consistent with statewide data showing that white defendants are less likely to go to prison following a conviction in Superior Court. Black defendants are more likely than whites or Hispanics to serve their sentences in a state-level institution—a prison or a CYA facility.

Over the entire sample, the probability of receiving a prison sentence if arrested for robbery and convicted (of some crime) in Superior Court was 0.40. Of those who were convicted in Superior Court, 68 percent were convicted of robbery (in some form); 8 percent of aggravated assault; 17 percent of burglary/theft; and 6 percent were convicted of some other miscellaneous offense. There were no racial differences in the type of conviction offense.

Multiple regression analyses with these data permitted us to control simultaneously for the other factors and look at the independent effect of race on the probability of receiving a prison sentence, once convicted.[8] The following independent variables were included in the regression equation:

---

[8]We were not able to use a regression model prior to this point because most of the offender characteristics (e.g., prior record) were recorded only for defendants reaching the Superior Court.

- Current conviction crime type
- Prior criminal record
- Defendant's age
- Defendant's race
- Defendant's current criminal status (e.g., on parole, probation)

Appendix A reproduces the complete regression results, which show that several factors are statistically related to the probability of receiving a prison sentence, once convicted in Superior Court:

- The older the defendant, the more likely he was to be sentenced to prison.
- The more serious the conviction crime, the more likely the defendant was to get a prison sentence.
- People on conditional status (e.g., parole, probation) were more likely to be sentenced to prison.
- People with prior prison records were more likely to be sentenced to prison.
- Most important for our study, when all other factors (available to us) were controlled, black defendants had a statistically significant higher chance of going to prison than whites or Hispanics.

LENGTH OF COURT-IMPOSED SENTENCE

Our analyses of the OBTS data yielded evidence of racial disparities in post-arrest release rates and in type of sentence imposed. The latter, especially, seems to substantiate charges that the criminal justice system does sentence minorities to prison more often than it does whites. But what of *sentence length*? Critics have also repeatedly claimed that judges sentence minorities to longer sentences. Although the scope of the study did not permit us to analyze all aspects of case processing in all three states, it did allow us to analyze and compare length of court-imposed sentence. Considering the seriousness of the issue, we preferred to use the RIS data rather than limit the findings to one state.

To establish the minimum and maximum sentence imposed by the court for each inmate who completed the RIS questionnaire, we consulted his official corrections records. We used this information in separate regression analyses for the three states to assess possible racial disparities in those sentences.[9] The regression models controlled for

---

[9]The complete regression results are in Appendix B. They were similar whether we used minimum or maximum sentence, or their logarithms, as the dependent variable.

race, age, type of conviction crime, and number of previous juvenile and adult incarcerations. In all three states, we found that prior criminal record was not significantly related to *length* of court-imposed sentence. However, sentence length was significantly related to age and type of conviction crime. Further, the regression results indicate that, controlling for the defendant's age, conviction crime, and prior record, race made a difference in each state.

Although the relative lengths are not consistent for particular groups or states, these findings support charges that minorities receive longer sentences. In all three states, minority status alone accounted for an additional 1 to 7 months in sentence length.[10] (See Table 3.6.)

Table 3.6

ADDITIONAL MONTHS IMPOSED BY COURT
FOR MINORITY DEFENDANTS

State	Blacks	Hispanics
California	+1.4 months	+6.5 months*
Michigan	+7.2 months*	(sample too small to be included in regression)
Texas	+3.7 months	+2.0 months

*Statistically significant in regression analysis.

CONCLUSIONS AND IMPLICATIONS

From the comparative analysis of the total OBTS data for 1980, the more detailed analysis of the data on robbery defendants in Los Angeles County, and the RIS data on court-imposed sentence length, a paradoxical pattern emerges. Whites are evidently treated more

---

The regression results reproduced use the minimum sentence length as the dependent variable.

[10]We discuss the effect of sentence imposed on time actually served in Sec. V.

severely than blacks or Hispanics until the sentencing stage. White suspects are more likely to be arrested on warrant than on view, more likely to have the case accepted by the DA, and more likely to be formally charged with felonies or misdemeanors. After that point, however, the picture changes.

Once arraigned on felony charges, the races have a roughly equal chance of being prosecuted on those charges in Superior Court and about an equal chance of being convicted. Whites have a slightly higher conviction rate for felonies, but they are also more likely than minorities to plea bargain—and, by definition, plea bargaining guarantees some kind of conviction. Hispanic and black defendants are more likely to be tried by judge or jury.

After conviction, the system treats blacks and Hispanics more severely than it does whites. If they are convicted of misdemeanor charges, blacks and Hispanics are much more likely to go to jail, while whites are more likely to receive probation. If convicted of felony charges, blacks and Hispanics are more likely than whites to receive prison sentences. In either case, they are likely to receive longer sentences.

It is possible that this apparent discrimination is actually a factor of racial differences in plea bargaining. Although white defendants give up their chances of acquittal by plea bargaining, the plea bargain guarantees them a reduction in charge and/or lighter sentences. By going to trial, blacks and Hispanics keep open the possibility of acquittal, but there is evidence that sentencing is more severe for judge or jury trials (California Legislature, 1980). We discuss this question at greater length in the final section.

If what we have discovered in analyses of the OBTS and RIS data is discrimination, why should it operate in this apparently inconsistent fashion, treating white suspects more severely at the early stages of the process and minorities more severely at the later stages? If treatment severity is based on prior criminal record and violence of the offense, we would expect more severe treatment for violent offenders with serious prior records—but we would expect it to be consistent throughout the criminal justice process.

It is possible that minorities receive less severe treatment after arrest because the police are quicker to assume probable cause where minorities are concerned, but many arrestees are released when the grounds for arrest prove insufficient. That conjecture draws some credibility from the fact that the police obtain warrants to arrest whites more often than they do to arrest minority suspects. In short, they overarrest minorities relative to the number of crimes minorities actually commit. If so, the lower charging rates for minorities are ironically consistent with the harsher sentencing. Both may represent discrimination against minorities at these two key decision points.

The OBTS and RIS data do not allow us to resolve these questions. However, the RIS provides insights into the pre-arrest and post-sentencing experience of prisoners. By looking at these data, we learned a great deal more about possible discrimination in the criminal justice system from arrest through release from prison.

IV. ANALYZING RACIAL DIFFERENCES IN CRIMES COMMITTED AND ARREST RATES

Research has not been able to establish incontrovertible evidence for or against discrimination in arrests, largely because the necessary information is not readily available. To estimate whether minorities are overarrested *relative to the number of crimes they actually commit*, analysts need comparable "pre-arrest" information for both whites and minorities: prevalence of crime types committed, incidence of crime or crime commission rates, and the probability of arrest. While official records provide information on the crimes for which offenders are arrested and convicted, they provide no information on how many other crimes and types of crimes these people commit; and they tell nothing, of course, about the race and criminal activities of offenders who are never arrested.

The difficulty of obtaining pre-arrest information impedes research on possible discrimination in arrests and the overrepresentation of minorities in prisons. As a National Institute of Corrections conference on racial discrimination concluded, "There appears to be little payoff in understanding the incremental contribution of each processing level to differential incarceration rates given that the major variance involves *prearrest factors*" (National Institute of Corrections, 1980).

To overcome this obstacle we used data from the Rand Inmate Survey (RIS) to answer four questions about the prisoners in the sample:

- Are there racial differences in the *kinds* of crimes that prisoners committed before arrest?
- Are there racial differences in the *range* of crime types they reported committing?
- Are there racial differences in crime commission *rates* reported in the sample?
- Are there racial differences in the *probability* that a single crime will result in arrest?

The answers indicate that, at least for our sample states, there is no consistent evidence that minorities are overarrested—in relation to white offenders or to the number of crimes they actually commit.

FINDINGS FROM THE RAND INMATE SURVEY

Eliciting the Data

Our purposes were to estimate separately the range of crime types committed by the racial groups, the incidence of crime or crime commission rates for individuals in those groups, and then to estimate the probability that a single crime would result in arrest for members of that group. To collect the necessary data, the RIS asked respondents to report on the number of crimes of various types that they had committed in a specified period, and what proportion of these crimes resulted in arrest. To begin, each respondent filled in a calendar covering a one-to-two-year period preceding the arrest that led to his current imprisonment. The calendar then showed for each month whether he was incarcerated, hospitalized, or on the street. From the calendar, the offender could then determine his "street months"—all questions about his criminal behavior referred constantly to his "street months." (The average for street months was 15.) He was then asked whether or not he had committed the crimes of burglary, business or personal robbery, grand theft, auto theft, forgery, fraud, drug dealing, or assault. These behaviors were described in ordinary language rather than in legal terms. After answering "yes" that he had committed a given type of crime, say, burglary, during the study period, the respondent was asked to tell how many burglaries he had committed by specifying a range, either "1 to 10" or "11 or more." If the range was "1 to 10," he was asked, "How many?" If the range was "11 or more," he was led through a sequence of questions about the number of months in which he committed burglary and his daily, weekly, or monthly rate of commission.[1]

From that information, we estimated the respondent's annualized crime commission rate. The annualized rate can be interpreted as the number of crimes committed per year of free time, since it takes into account the length of time the respondent was incarcerated during his measurement period. For example, if a respondent's measurement period lasted 14 months, of which he spent five months in jail, and he committed six burglaries, his annualized crime rate would be:

$$\text{Annualized crime rate} = (6 \text{ burglaries}) \times (12 \text{ months})/(14\text{-}5) \text{ months}$$

$$= 72/9 = 8.0 \text{ burglaries/year}$$

---

[1]See Chaiken and Chaiken (1982) for a description of the exact wording of the crime-related questions and a complete explanation of the manner in which the "study period" was calculated. Peterson et al. (1982) describe the pretests that led to this choice of questionnaire format.

Before we present our analysis, it is important to point out the limitations of the RIS as a means of calculating crime rates and of detecting racial differences in these rates. All the men who completed our survey were in prison; the sample was chosen to represent each state's male prison population. It is not appropriate, therefore, to view these crime rates as applicable to offenders in the community. They refer only to a cohort of incoming prisoners in the states chosen for this study. Selection effects and other factors cause these rates to be substantially higher than those for "typical" offenders (Rolph, Chaiken, and Houchens, 1981). This is an important limitation, and must be kept in mind in interpreting the results. Our results speak only to crime rates and racial differences apparent in the crimes committed by incarcerated males in a recent period preceding their current imprisonment.

Findings

Racial Differences in Range of Crime Types. Table 4.1 presents the percentages of each racial group that reported committing a particular crime *at least once* during the study period.

In the sample, the data revealed some differences in the kinds of crime the different races committed. In general:

- More Hispanics reported committing personal crimes—both personal robberies and aggravated assault.
- More whites and Hispanics reported involvement in both drug dealing and burglary.
- Significantly more whites committed forgery, theft of credit cards, and auto thefts.

Table 4.1 also indicates that certain crimes were committed by a very large percentage of the prisoners while other crimes were less "popular." Over half (52 percent) of the respondents report committing at least one burglary in the 12 to 24 months preceding their current imprisonment; 43 percent reported dealing in drugs, and 40 percent reported some theft. However, only about one-fourth reported doing a robbery (either of a person or business), and less than one-fifth reported involvement in frauds or swindles.

Crime Commission Rates. The data enabled us to compute the annualized crime commission rate for each racial group; these rates are technically referred to as "lambdas."

Six years ago, virtually no information was available on individual rates of criminal activity. Estimates of average offense rates, which were based on various methods of estimation from aggregate crime

Table 4.1

PERCENT OF PRISONERS COMMITTING CRIME, BY CRIME TYPE AND RACE
(Three States Combined)

Crime Type	White (521)	Black (718)	Hispanic (141)	Chi-Square	All Races Combined
Burglary	58	47	60	<.001	52
Business robbery	25	24	26	NS	24
Personal robbery	20	24	32	<.01	23
Theft (not auto)	44	37	42	NS	40
Auto theft	32	19	26	<.001	24
Forgery/credit cards	29	19	20	<.001	23
Frauds/swindles	14	19	14	NS	16
Drug deals	53	35	53	<.001	43
Aggravated assault	37	26	40	<.001	32
All personal crimes[a] combined	51	45	56	<.05	49
All property crimes[b] combined (excluding drugs)	48	34	18	NS	77
All crimes combined (excluding drugs)	84	78	82	<.05	81

[a]Personal crimes include business robbery, personal robbery, and aggravated assault.

[b]Property crimes include burglary, theft, auto theft, forgery credit cards, frauds, and swindles.

and arrest data, ranged from less than one felony per year (Greenberg, 1975) to five or more (Shinnar and Shinnar, 1975). Petersilia's (1977) study of 49 robbers estimated that this group averaged about 20 felonies per year. Subsequently, Peterson and Braiker (1981) and Blumstein and Cohen (1979) developed estimates for specific offense types based on self-reports and arrest histories, respectively.

Table 4.2 shows the mean, median, and 90th percentile offense rates among active offenders, broken down by race. This table shows dramatically the uniqueness of the RIS crime commission data: These averages are quite unstable. This results from the fact that even among prisoners, the vast majority of those who commit any particular type of crime do so rather infrequently.

Table 4.2

ANNUALIZED CRIME COMMISSION RATES FOR ACTIVE OFFENDERS

(Three States Combined)

Crime Type	White			Black			Hispanic		
	Mean	Median	90th %	Mean	Median	90th %	Mean	Median	90th %
Burglary	75	8	361	25	4	154	57	6	308
Business robbery	15	4	76	9	5	30	29	4	159
Personal robbery	12	4	55	17	4	99	9	4	41
Theft (not auto)	61	9	277	89	6	456	80	11	387
Auto theft	11	3	48	43	3	276	12	3	63
Forgery/credit cards	38	6	198	31	4	193	7	3	25
Frauds/swindles	27	7	147	53	5	280	5	4	16
Drug deals	703	156	3427	786	92	4123	420	78	1824
Aggravated assault	5	3	14	3	2	8	4	3	14

NOTE: The mean, median, and 90th percentile refer to those respondents who commit the crime in question; 50 percent commit the crime at rates above the median, and 10 percent at rates above the 90th percentile.

This finding is consistent with previous research.[2] In any subgroup of offenders (other than one based on crime rates) most members will commit none or only a few of each particular crime, but a small number will commit the crime at very high rates. For each of the crime types we studied, the distributions were similar, all having a heavy concentration near zero and a long, thin tail.

These skewed distributions applied to each of the crime types, any combination of crimes, and to each of the three racial groups. Figure 4.1 illustrates the shape of the robbery distribution. Similar graphs applied to the rest of the crime types as well. All of the distributions have a heavy concentration near zero and a long, thin tail. Personal and business robberies have almost identical distributions, and despite substantial statistical differences, the shape of the distributions for robbery appears similar to the shape for burglary, auto theft, and forgery/credit cards. Theft other than auto also appears similar to these, but at twice the scale. Two crime types appear visually to be substantially different: assault has a very short tail, and drug dealing has a very long tail. The sum of all study crimes other than drug dealing takes its shape primarily from the theft crimes, which constitute the largest component (Chaiken and Chaiken, 1982).

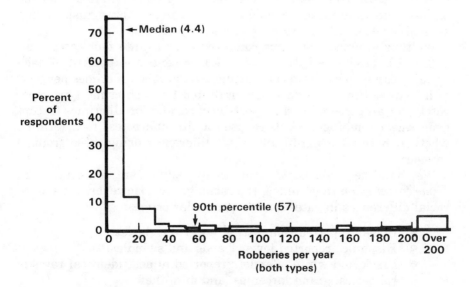

Fig. 4.1—Robbery commission rates: the number of crimes committed per year of street time

---

[2]Petersilia et al. (1978); Peterson and Braiker (1981); Chaiken and Chaiken (1982).

The extreme skewness of the distributions presents particular problems for standard statistics. In characterizing these distributions, the median is a poor descriptor because its magnitude gives little hint of the crime commission rates of the most active offenders. The mean, too, is a poor descriptor because it is unduly sensitive to the values of a few outlier crime commission rates for the respondents who reported extremely high rates. Excluding these high values as outliers in the analysis is not satisfactory because the people with high crime-commission propensities are the very offenders who warrant the greatest policy interest. And the 90th percentile represents the rates of only the most serious offenders.[3]

Our concerns about response validity and the difficulties created by these skewed distributions caused us to treat the offense rates as categories rather than continuous variables. We believe that the offense rate data are useful in providing information about the *general* level of criminal activity. However, we are uncertain whether the respondents who reported committing 10 or 20 robberies actually committed that exact number. However, respondents who reported 10 or 20 robberies probably did commit appreciably more robberies than those who reported one or two (assuming that both are attempting to provide accurate information). This reasoning suggested to us that the offense rate information should be used only to distinguish among several levels of offense rates, i.e., low, medium, or high.

We thus grouped the crime commission rates into four categories: 1–3, 4–10, 11–20, and 21+. Table 4.3 presents the percent of each racial group who reported committing that number of crimes per year of his street time. The data are presented for each crime type separately, for all personal and property crimes, and for all crimes (except drug sales) combined. We then used a chi-square test to determine whether there were significant racial differences using these grouped categories.

We found few *consistent*, statistically significant, differences in *crime commission rates* among the racial groups. However, there were racial differences in rates for two particular crimes:

- Blacks reported committing fewer burglaries.
- Hispanics reported fewer frauds and swindles.
- Black and white offenders reported almost identical rates of robberies, grand larcenies, and auto thefts.
- Black and white offenders committed a greater number of drug deals than Hispanics, although these differences were not statistically significant.

---

[3]See Rolph, Chaiken, and Houchens (1981) for a complete discussion of the statistical problems resulting from these unique distributions.

Table 4.3

DISTRIBUTION OF ANNUALIZED CRIME COMMISSION RATES FOR RESPONDENTS WHO COMMIT THE CRIMES[a]
(States Combined)

Crime Type	Crime Rate				Chi-Square
	1-3	4-10	11-20	21+	
Burglary					
White	32	22	8	38	
Black	48	23	7	22	
Hispanic	35	24	11	30	<.05
All races	39	23	8	30	
Business robbery					
White	50	21	11	19	
Black	38	34	11	17	
Hispanic	38	28	9	25	NS
All races	43	28	10	18	
Personal robbery					
White	44	32	5	19	
Black	48	30	5	17	
Hispanic	38	40	12	10	NS
All races	45	32	6	17	
Theft (not auto)					
White	25	28	8	39	
Black	30	30	5	35	
Hispanic	24	25	15	35	NS
All races	27	29	7	37	
Auto theft					
White	51	26	7	16	
Black	52	26	2	20	
Hispanic	53	25	6	16	NS
All races	52	26	5	17	
Forgery/credit cards					
White	34	25	12	29	
Black	50	22	5	23	
Hispanic	50	34	0	16	NS
All races	42	25	8	25	
Drug deals[b]					
White	33	6	14	47	
Black	44	4	8	43	
Hispanic	43	5	17	34	NS
All races	38	5	12	44	

Table 4.3—continued

Crime Type	1-3	4-10	11-20	21+	Chi-Square
Aggravated assault[c]					
White	31	36	33	--	
Black	38	40	21	--	
Hispanic	37	26	37	--	NS
All races	34	37	29	--	
Fraud/swindles					
White	29	29	16	26	
Black	39	31	4	26	
Hispanic	39	50	6	6	<.05
All races	36	32	8	24	
All personal crimes combined					
White	26	28	12	34	
Black	49	22	8	22	
Hispanic	31	28	8	33	
All races	34	26	10	30	NS
All property crimes (except drugs)					
White	14	12	8	66	
Black	12	23	13	52	
Hispanic	15	15	18	51	
All races	13	16	11	59	NS

[a]N=1380. Respondents reported activity for a varying number of months during the window period. The mean number of months offenders were reporting on was 15 months.

The entries are the percent of the sample who were "active" in the specific crime type (i.e., reported committing at least one crime of that type in the window period).

[b]Categories for drug sales are: <20, 21-50, 51-200, more than 200.

[c]The categories for aggravated assault are 1, 2-5, more than 5.

That last finding permits a precise illustration of the difference between range of criminality and incidence of crime. The findings on *range* indicate that more Hispanics than blacks reported being involved in at least one drug deal. However, the annualized crime rates, which represent *incidence*, indicate that once involved in drug dealing, blacks did more of it than Hispanics did.

In combining all the personal crimes or all the property crimes, we found no statistically significant differences among the races. However, when *all* the crimes (except drug dealing) were combined, we found that white respondents reported committing crimes at the highest rates, followed by blacks, and then Hispanics. This result appears to reflect the fact that whites reported committing a greater number of property crimes. Consequently, even though these differences were not statistically significant within the property crime category, when the property and personal crimes were combined, whites had higher rates primarily because of their greater involvement in burglary, forgery, and fraud.

After closely examining the data in a number of different ways— means, medians, 90th percentiles, etc.—we found no strong evidence of any consistent, significant racial differences in crime commission rates. That is, *once an offender became involved in a particular crime type, the rate at which he committed that crime while on the street was quite similar among the races.*

PROBABILITY OF ARREST

Although these findings establish that the incidence of crime, once the person is involved, does not differ appreciably among the races, they still do not negate the possibility that the police overarrest minorities. It has been suggested that even if minorities commit about the same number of crimes as whites, they are more likely to be arrested.

Research on this issue has discovered some evidence that race affects the probability of arrest. In a study that is consistent with our OBTS findings, Hepburn (1976) concluded that "nonwhites are more likely than whites to be arrested under circumstances that will not constitute sufficient grounds for prosecution." Other studies have found that the decision to arrest appears to depend partly on nonlegal variables such as the suspect's attitude, race, and demeanor (Piliavin and Briar, 1964). Arrest has also been found to depend on the complainant's attitude (Black, 1970). Black complainants are more likely than white to want suspects arrested, and because crimes were generally intraracial, this can operate to the disadvantage of black suspects (Collins, 1977). Finally, Forslund (1969) found that blacks were charged with more offenses per arrest than whites.

It is difficult to estimate the probability of arrest for different subgroups of the population. An arrest probability is calculated by dividing the number of crimes of a particular type that an offender committed by the number of times he was arrested over the same period for that crime. As we have seen, that kind of information is difficult to come by. Consequently, very few attempts have been made to calculate arrest probabilities and compare them among racial groups.

In Petersilia et al. (1978) and Peterson and Braiker (1981), arrest probabilities were derived from prisoner self-reports.[4] The sample in the Peterson and Braiker study was large enough to explore racial differences. They found that "There was some evidence to suggest that whites commit more crimes, and that white offenders have consistently lower probabilities of arrest than do either blacks or Mexican-Americans. This is particularly striking for armed robbery and burglary. Minority offenders are two or three times more likely to be arrested for an armed robbery or burglary than are whites." (Peterson and Braiker, 1981, p. 62.)

Research has repeatedly shown that criminals face a rather low chance of being arrested. Blumstein and Cohen (1979) estimated the probability of arrest for robbery to be 0.07; for assault, 0.11; and for burglary, 0.05. Peterson and Braiker's (1981) estimates were in reasonable accord with these; they found further that the probability of arrest for forgery was 0.06, and for drug sales, 0.002. Previous drug-crime research has estimated the likelihood of arrest, given the commission of an offense, at less than one percent (Inciardi and Chambers, 1972; Collins et al., 1982).

The arrest probabilities calculated from our Inmate Survey were ultimately quite consistent with previous research.[5] Table 4.4 lists the average probabilities of arrest by race.

---

[4]It is not absolutely necessary to have self-reports from offenders; an alternative is to "model" the arrest process by using information on the number of crimes reported and the number of offenders arrested. This approach is used by Blumstein and Cohen (1979). Both self-reports and the modeling approach undoubtedly involve errors, due, respectively, to self-report biases and assumptions about the arrest process. Nevertheless, the Blumstein and Cohen results are strikingly similar to those derived using offender self-reports.

[5]In our survey, each inmate who reported committing a crime (during the window period) was asked whether any of his crimes (specified by crime type) resulted in arrest. He was also asked to specify the number of arrests that occurred. For example, persons who reported robbing a business during the window period were then asked, "How many of these robberies were you arrested for? (Include all of the times you were arrested for robbing a business even if you were charged with something else.)"

Table 4.4

Probability of Arrest by Race
(Three States Combined)

Crime Type	White	Black	Hispanic	All Races Combined
Burglary	.04	.09	.06	.06
Business robbery	.28	.15	.28	.21
Personal robbery	.10	.20	.18	.16
Theft (not auto)	.02	.03	.03	.02
Auto theft	.09	.16	.09	.11
Forgery/credit cards	.05	.04	.06	.05
Frauds/swindles	.02	.01	.02	.01
Drug deals	.000	.001	.000	.001
Aggravated assault	.20	.26	.32	.24

However, as with the crime commission data, the arrest probability data were not normally distributed. The crime commission data showed that most offenders committed one or two crimes of a particular type, while a small number of offenders committed hundreds. The skewed distribution forced us to collapse the crime rates into categories in order to determine whether there were racial differences.

A similar problem existed for the arrest probabilities. While it might seem desirable to compute an "average" arrest probability for each race, and then compare the averages, such statistics are inappropriate. For example, suppose that five offenders report committing business robberies during our window period. Four of the five report two robberies each, while the fifth reports committing 25. Further, suppose that only one robbery ended in arrest. To compute an average arrest probability, we would divide 1 by the total of 32 robberies, yielding a probability of 0.03. The one offender who reported committing 25 robberies dominated the statistic.

We consulted several statisticians about the appropriate methods to use in testing for racial differences with such skewed distributions. We needed to compute statistics that would reduce the influence of the very high rate offenders. The best procedure seemed to be to use the categorized crime commission rates—low, medium, high, and very high—and then compute arrest probabilities within each category. The numbers within each cell could then be interpreted as the probability of arrest for offenders with different (grouped) crime commission rates.

Table 4.5 presents the results, which illustrate the uniqueness of the arrest probability data. For most of the crime types, the probability of arrest is much higher for persons who committed only a few crimes, and decreases as the number of crimes increases.

Overall, we found no strong evidence of consistent racial differences in the probability of being arrested for any of the crimes we studied. In a few selected instances, there were statistically significant differences. For example, in personal robberies the data show that minority offenders falling in either the 4–10 or 11–20 crime commission category had a 10 to 20 percent higher chance of being arrested. Whites who committed frauds at a rate of 4 to 10 or 11 to 20 had about a 10 percent higher chance of being arrested than blacks or Hispanics. In combining all of the personal crimes, or all of the property crimes, we find few significant racial differences.

In general, in looking at any of the four crime commission categories or any of the eleven crime types, the probability of arrest does not differ by more than 10 percentage points among the races. If there were real racial differences in arrest probabilities, we would expect to see larger differences, and in a consistent direction (whites consistently lower than blacks or Hispanics). Our data, however, are not this obvious. The rates for the three races are quite similar, overall, within the specific crime categories. When differences do result, the lower rates occur sometimes for whites, sometimes for blacks, and sometimes for Hispanics. From this data, we then conclude that there are no apparent racial differences in the probability of suffering an arrest, given that an offender committed one of our studied offenses.

CONCLUSIONS

The RIS data suggest that, relative to the prevalence and incidence of crime among white and minority offenders, the police do not generally overarrest minorities. There are some racial differences in the types of crimes committed, and some crimes for which each racial group seems to have a higher probability of arrest. However, these differences are not consistent—or, at least, not consistently, statistically, significant. This leads us to conclude that the high release rate for black and Hispanic suspects in the OBTS data has some other explanation than discrimination at the point of arrest. We discuss the possibilities in the final section of the report.

Although the RIS data offer no firm explanation for the high release rate, they counter the suspicion of discrimination in arrest rates, at least for the study states. In the next section, we examine them for evidence of racial differences in treatment at the corrections level.

Table 4.5

PROBABILITY OF ARREST BY RACE OF OFFENDER AND NUMBER OF CRIMES COMMITTED

(Three States Combined)

Crime and Race	Annual Crime Commission Rate			
	1-3	4-10	11-20	21+
Burglary				
White	.27	.21	.10	.01
Black	.43	.20	.08	.01
Hispanic	.32	.19	.13	.00
All	.36	.21	.10	.01
Chi-square	<.05	NS	NS	NS
Business Robbery				
White	.44	.35	.13	.05
Black	.42	.19	.09	.01
Hispanic	.40	.26	.15	.03
All	.43	.23	.11	.03
Chi-square	NS	<.001	NS	NS
Personal Robbery				
White	.41	.09	.04	.00
Black	.35	.26	.12	.00
Hispanic	.33	.22	.27	.01
All	.36	.19	.11	.00
Chi-square	NS	<.001	<.005	NS
Auto Theft				
White	.24	.15	.15	.00
Black	.40	.15	.14	.00
Hispanic	.29	.14	.07	.00
All	.31	.15	.13	.00
Chi-square	<.05	NS	NS	NS
Fraud				
White	.00	.08	.10	.00
Black	.05	.03	.00	.00
Hispanic	.06	.00	.11	.00
All	.04	.04	.07	.00
Chi-square	NS	NS	NS	NS
Forgery				
White	.17	.10	.09	.00
Black	.23	.10	.04	.00
Hispanic	.17	.04	--	.00
All	.19	.09	.08	.00
Chi-square	NS	NS	NS	NS

Table 4.5—continued

Crime and Race	Annual Crime Commission Rate			
	1-3	4-10	11-20	21+
Drug Deals[a]				
White	.05	.00	.00	.00
Black	.05	.01	.00	.00
Hispanic	.08	.00	.00	.00
All	.05	.01	.00	.00
Chi-square	NS	NS	NS	NS
Theft (not auto)				
White	.23	.12	.06	.00
Black	.37	.14	.13	.00
Hispanicc	.20	.18	.07	.00
All	.30	.13	.09	.00
Chi-square	<.05	NS	<.05	NS
Personal Crime				
White	.39	.23	.17	.02
Black	.36	.21	.16	.00
Hispanic	.45	.30	.09	.03
All	.38	.22	.16	.01
Chi-square	NS	NS	NS	NS
Property Crimes (excluding drugs)				
White	.35	.37	.22	.01
Black	.69	.32	.20	.00
Hispanic	.61	.28	.19	.00
All	.56	.33	.21	.00
Chi-square	<.001	NS	NS	NS
All Crimes (excluding drugs)				
White	.42	.39	.21	.02
Black	.65	.36	.26	.00
Hispanic	.47	.45	.24	.00
All	.55	.38	.24	.00
Chi-square	<.001	NS	NS	NS

NOTE: NS = not significant.

[a]Drug sale categories were <21, 21-50, 51-200, 201+.

V. RACIAL DIFFERENCES IN CORRECTIONS AND TIME SERVED

From arrest to sentencing, the system duly records most major decisions involving offenders. Consequently, it is rather easy to see racial differences in handling—even if it is still difficult to tell whether those differences signify discrimination. However, once a person is sentenced to prison, he is potentially subject to many decisions that are not systematically, if ever, recorded. Prison guards and staff make decisions that strongly influence the quality of an offender's time in prison, and parole boards and other corrections officials decide how long that time lasts. The possibility of discrimination enters into all these decisions, but the length of time served is the only one certain to be recorded. In other words, corrections is a closed world in which discrimination could flourish.

That charge has frequently been brought against the system. In a recent report, the National Minority Advisory Council (1980) concluded that corrections discriminates against minorities in awarding good-time credits, allocating treatment and work programs, punishing infractions, and granting parole. Even if we put aside the questions of justice and equity raised by that charge, the steady increase of racial problems in prison makes it imperative to examine the treatment that different races receive in prison and at parole.

Using data from official records, where available, and the RIS, we analyzed the in-prison treatment and length of sentence served for our study sample. We found some racial differences for participation in work and treatment programs, but they were largely determined by the prisoners, not by guards or staff. If prisoners needed and wanted to participate in programs, they generally could, regardless of race; and the rate of participation for major programs was not significantly biased racially.

However, it was evident that although minorities received equal treatment in prison, they did not when it came time for release. Controlling for factors that could affect the release decision (including participation in prison programs and prison violence), we found consistent evidence that race made a difference. In Texas, all other things held equal, blacks and Hispanics consistently served longer sentences than whites for the same crimes. In California, minority inmates also served longer sentences, but that was largely determined by the length of sentence originally imposed. Michigan manifested an interesting reversal. Although blacks received longer court-imposed sentences than whites, they wound up serving about the same time. In Michigan, then, parole decisions seemed to "favor" blacks—that is, blacks evidently served less of their original sentences than whites did.

PARTICIPATION IN PRISON PROGRAMS

The Research Background

There is little research on the breadth of treatment programs employed in prison and the racial or other characteristics of prisoners who participate. Reanalyzing data from *1974 Survey of Inmates in State Correctional Facilities*, Petersilia determined that, nationwide, 22 percent of the inmates needed treatment for alcohol rehabilitation, 23 percent needed drug rehabilitation, 31 percent needed job training, and 68 percent needed further education. The study also determined that about one in five inmates with a serious need participated in a corresponding treatment program while in prison and that, nationwide, 40 percent of inmates participated in some treatment program while in prison (Petersilia, 1980).

The study also found some racial differences in treatment: Whites and nonblack minorities were more likely to receive needed alcohol treatment, but less likely to receive needed drug treatment. Twenty-two percent of the whites with serious alcohol problems received treatment but only 12 percent of the blacks. Black inmates, however, participated in drug programs more often than either whites or other minorities. With respect to job training and education programs, the "other" minority group—primarily Hispanics—had a much lower participation rate (Petersilia, 1980, p. 130).

To identify possible discrimination in treatment, one must look at some complex interrelationships, as well as data on who participates and why. To analyze these relationships, we addressed the following questions:

- What proportion of prison inmates need treatment in education, vocational training, alcohol rehabilitation, and drug rehabilitation? Are there racial differences in need?
- What proportion of inmates who need treatment participate in the appropriate treatment program? Are there racial differences in the proportion receiving needed treatment?
- When minorities fail to participate in needed programs, do their reasons differ from those of other inmates (e.g., staff discouraged participation)?

- How do the inmates of different races assess the effects of the programs they participated in?
- Do fewer minority inmates hold prison jobs?
- Are there racial differences in work experiences, evaluations of work, and reasons for not working?

The data necessary to answer these questions were provided by the inmate survey and information from official corrections files. Our "need" categories were determined in part from information recorded during the inmate's intake evaluation. Thus, all results in this section are based on those inmates whose surveys could be matched with their official records ("Survey Plus Official Records" sample equals 1214 persons).[1]

A word of caution in interpreting our results: Our sample was selected to include people at random points in their current terms, not interviewed at the end of their prison terms. If inmates received treatment only toward the end of their terms, one would expect the program participation rates to increase as proportion of sentence served increased. In this case, sampling offenders at random points in their term would underestimate the percentage of the population who eventually became involved in programs. However, prior research indicates that programs are generally available to all inmates who wish to participate, regardless of sentence length or time served. Only in vocational training programs do participation rates increase slightly as the inmate nears the end of his sentence (Petersilia, 1980). Analysis of the RIS showed no association between the number of months an inmate had been in prison and his participation rate in either prison treatment or work programs. We therefore did not control for months served in the subsequent analysis.

Treatment Emphasis in Different States

The answers to our research questions must be viewed from the wider perspective of each state's overall inmate participation and main treatment type. Inmate participation in programs and work assignments varied across states:

- In Michigan, 80 percent of the inmates were in a major treatment program, an additional 5 percent in other prison programs, 5 percent in work assignments only, and 10 percent were idle.[2]

---

[1]See Petersilia and Honig (1980) for the specific questions asked in the survey.
[2]Major programs are education, vocational training, and alcohol and drug rehabili-

- In Texas, 66 percent were in a major program, 11 percent in other programs, 11 percent in work assignments only, and 12 percent were idle.
- In California, 64 percent were in a major treatment program, 14 percent in other minor prison programs, 13 percent had work assignments only, and 9 percent were idle.
- Basic adult education and vocational training are the main treatment program types in each of these states. Participation in alcohol rehabilitation programs varied from 11 to 20 percent of the inmates surveyed.
- Only in Michigan did a nontrivial proportion, 28 percent, of the inmates participate in a drug rehabilitation program.[3]

Needs Vs. Participation in Programs

Although a prisoner may need treatment of a certain type, he may not necessarily get to participate in the appropriate program. As we saw, some critics have charged that the system discriminates against minorities in allocating work and treatment assignments. One way of assessing that charge is to compare the proportions of different racial groups who need treatment with those who participate, and then to compare the participation rates of racial groups.

Criteria of Need. For prison staff, establishing an inmate's need for treatment involves complex, somewhat subjective considerations. However, our purposes required fairly simple, objective criteria, which we based on data available from the official records and the RIS. Our criteria for "high need" were:

> *Education:* less than 9th-grade education, as shown by the official corrections record; or reading level at or below 9th grade.

> *Vocational training:* no employment and no other legitimate activity (e.g., school attendance, military) during the "window" period (up to two years of street time) preceding the current term of imprisonment, as shown by Inmate Survey self-report.

> *Alcohol rehabilitation*: self-report of serious drinking problems during the window period.

---

tation. Other programs are psychological counseling, self-help groups, home visitations, etc. By idle, we mean that inmates were in neither work nor treatment programs.

[3]For a more complete discussion of these state differences, see Petersilia and Honig (1980).

Drug rehabilitation: self-report of daily use of hard drugs (i.e., heroin, barbiturates, amphetamines) during the window period.

Need Compared with Participation for All Inmates. Once each inmate was classified as to his degree of need for a particular form of treatment, we were able to determine how many inmates with a high need for treatment actually participated in a corresponding treatment program. Figure 5.1 shows the percentage in each state classified as having a high need, and the percentage of those with a high need who participated in appropriate treatment prior to the survey.

In all three states, need and participation were most closely matched for education. In Michigan, 71 percent of those with a high need for education had participated in an education program prior to the survey; in Texas, 59 percent; and in California, 45 percent.

In other programs, the match between high need and participation is progressively poorer. For vocational programs, only about 30 percent of the high-need inmates participated, prior to the survey, in all three states. Participation for alcohol also had a lower match with need: In all three states, about 30 percent of the population was classified as having a high need for treatment, but in Michigan only 37 percent of these participated; in Texas, 35 percent; and in California, 19 percent. In drug rehabilitation, there is even less correspondence between need and treatment received. In California and Texas, only about 5 percent of those with high need participated in a drug treatment program. Only in Michigan does there appear to be a serious attempt to involve inmates in drug programs: 55 percent of the high-need inmates participated.

Racial Differences in Treatment Need and Program Participation

Because of the sizable state differences in the participation rates, we were forced to analyze racial differences in each state separately. Michigan inmates participated more frequently in programs than inmates in the other states, and over half of the Michigan sample was black. If we combined all the states' results, we might find that blacks participate more frequently in all program types. We could then erroneously conclude that whites and Hispanics were being denied treatment, when in fact the result was reflecting state, as opposed to racial, differences.

An inmate's race and age have been repeatedly suggested by prison administrators as the factors most likely to affect the "match" be-

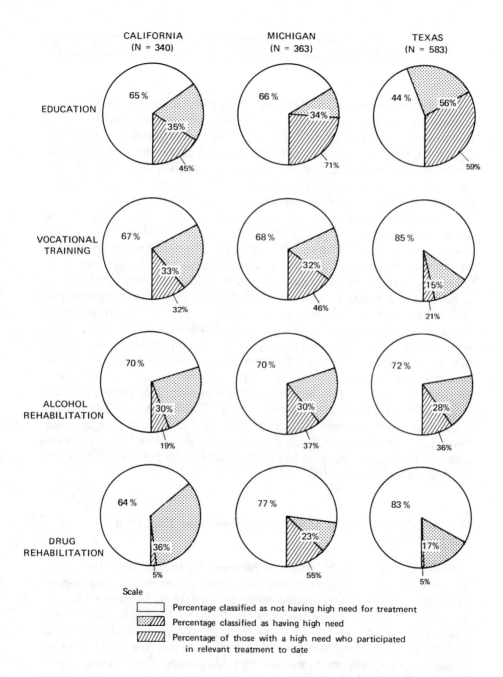

Fig. 5.1—Correspondence between high need for treatment and
treatment received

tween need and treatment received (see Petersilia and Honig, 1980). It may be that particular racial groups discourage participation in programs that are run by prison staff, or programs in which other racial groups are the most frequent participants. We explore these hypotheses below.

Education Programs. Figure 5.2 depicts the match between need and participation in education programs. In each state, a greater percentage of minority inmates than of whites were classified as having a high need. This was particularly true for Hispanics—78 percent of those in Texas had a "high need" for further education. In California and Michigan, however, race did not significantly affect the match between need and treatment received. But in Texas there was a statistically significant difference: Blacks received less treatment.

Vocational Training Programs. We were particularly interested in whether minorities met the criteria for need in vocational training more than whites did and, more important, whether race was associated with participation. In both California and Michigan, a disproportionate number of black inmates disclosed a high need, but race did not significantly affect participation. Across all states, equal proportions of blacks, whites, and Hispanics participated. (See Fig. 5.3.)

Alcohol Rehabilitation Programs. The three states exhibited highly significant differences among the races in the percentage needing alcohol rehabilitation, as shown in Fig. 5.4. In each instance, whites outweighed the others in need, with blacks being the least needful. It is also true, especially in California, that disproportionately fewer black inmates participate in alcohol rehabilitation programs.

The finding that blacks were underrepresented in alcohol treatment programs is consistent with the findings of earlier research (Petersilia, 1980). Using a nationwide prison sample, that study found that fewer black inmates have serious alcohol problems; but for those with problems, a relatively smaller proportion will be treated. It may be that alcohol problems are perceived as a white-class phenomenon, and the prison programs are predominantly made up of Anglo staff and participants. This situation may discourage black inmates from participating. As will be discussed below, the low rate of participation by high-need blacks does not seem to result from staff discrimination.

Drug Rehabilitation Programs. There was some limited evidence in each of the states that a larger percentage of white inmates had a higher need for drug treatment than blacks and Hispanics, but did not participate in programs to any greater degree (see Fig. 5.5).

Association of Other Inmate Characteristics with Program Need and Participation. We examined a number of other factors besides race—including age, time already served, commitment offense, career criminality, juvenile record, prior prison terms, etc.—

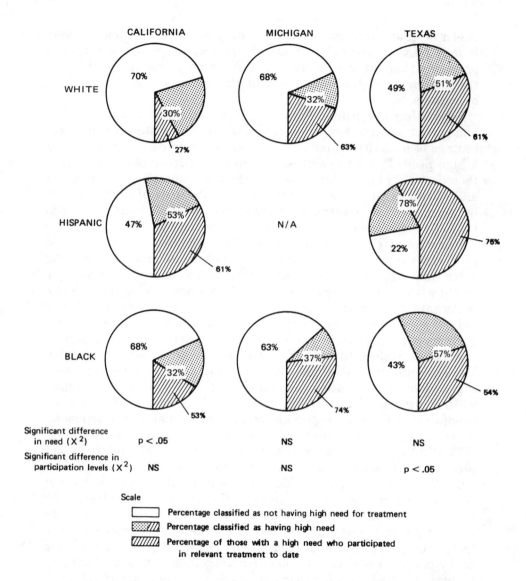

Fig. 5.2—Participation of high need inmates in education
programs, by race

57

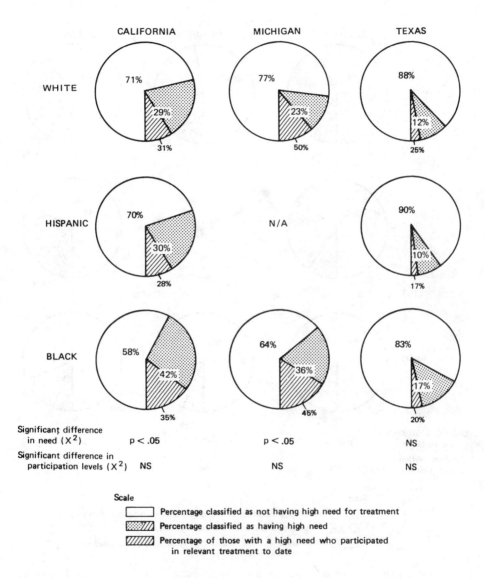

CALIFORNIA   MICHIGAN   TEXAS

WHITE

71%   29%   31%

77%   23%   50%

88%   12%   25%

HISPANIC

70%   30%   28%

N/A

90%   10%   17%

BLACK

58%   42%   35%

64%   36%   45%

83%   17%   20%

Significant difference in need (X^2) $p < .05$ $p < .05$ NS

Significant difference in participation levels (X^2)   NS   NS   NS

Scale

☐ Percentage classified as not having high need for treatment

▨ Percentage classified as having high need

▨ Percentage of those with a high need who participated in relevant treatment to date

Fig. 5.3—Participation of high need inmates in vocational training programs, by race

58

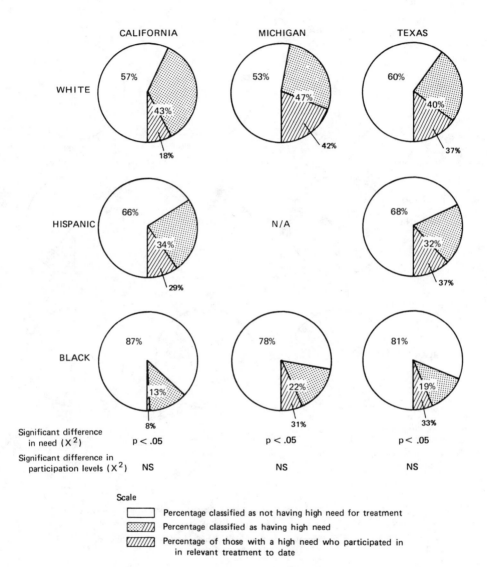

Fig. 5.4—Participation of high need inmates in alcohol
rehabilitation programs, by race

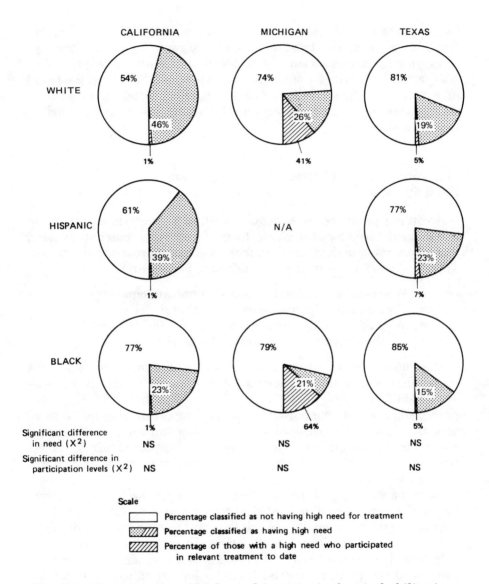

Fig. 5.5—Participation of high need inmates in drug rehabilitation
programs, by race

seeking to explain the association between need and participation. We found prison programs to be allocated quite randomly among inmates of varying ages, races, criminal histories, and sentence lengths. This was particularly true for education and vocational training. We found no evidence that inmates with these unique characteristics had more serious treatment needs or were participating less, in corresponding treatments.

Motivations for and Reactions to Program Participation

According to our criteria, about one-third of the prison population had an acute need for at least one form of treatment under study here, and about one-fourth of that number received appropriate treatment. These statistics raise important questions for research:

- What factors motivate inmates who participate?
- How do participants assess the results?
- Why do so many "high need" inmates fail to participate?
- Do the answers differ among the races?

The inmates surveyed were asked to rate on a four-point scale the importance of each of five reasons for their participating in the various rehabilitative programs. The results indicate that 40 to 60 percent cited "help me to make parole" as a very important reason; 15 to 20 percent said they participated to "break up prison boredom," about 10 percent to "be with friends," and 70 to 80 percent to "obtain the objectives of the program." There were no significant racial differences among the answers.

Participants were asked to assess how much each program had helped them in terms of adjusting to prison, reducing future criminality, dealing with personal problems, and obtaining a skill or education that would assist in future employment. Programs of all types were judged in those terms. For each type, about 20 percent of the participants said the program helped them "a lot" in adjusting to prison; about 50 percent said they had attained the intended goal of the program; and between 40 and 50 percent believe the programs would help them stay out of crime. Half of the participants in drug or alcohol programs said they had been helped in curtailing their dependency on these substances; less than 20 percent said these programs were of no help. As expected, the program rated the best aid in getting a job after release was vocational training.

Most germane to our interests are the reasons given by minorities for not participating in needed treatment programs. Are programs unavailable to them, does the staff discourage participation, or do inmates feel they do not need treatment?

We found that 65 percent of the inmates we classified as having a high need for alcohol rehabilitation did not participate because they did not believe they needed such a program. This is particularly surprising, because our criterion for need was the inmate's own assessment of whether he had an alcohol problem during the months prior to his imprisonment.

The same finding applied to all of the other programs except drug rehabilitation: Inmates in need of treatment simply chose not to participate. With drug rehabilitation, however, 33 percent of the inmates judged to have a high need said they did not participate because programs were unavailable. Some 8 to 19 percent of our high-need inmates were not in programs because they felt they were too busy.

We found no significant racial differences in all these reasons. Had discrimination existed, we would have expected to find a greater proportion of minorities reporting that "staff discouraged my participation." There was a slight but statistically insignificant tendency for white offenders to deny their problem more than minorities, claiming that "I don't need this program" for most of the program types studied.

Assessing Prison Work Assignments

We looked for any racial differences in work assignments, in reasons for not having a job, and in evaluations of the usefulness of jobs. The percentages of inmates who reported having a prison job were 59 percent in California, 45 percent in Michigan, and 58 percent in Texas. We found that a greater proportion of white inmates held prison jobs in both Texas and Michigan (statistically significant in both states). Black inmates, particularly in Texas, were less likely to hold a prison job. In California, no racial differences were evident.

There were interesting state differences in reasons that inmates gave for not having a job. In general, inmates without jobs do not appear to want them. In both California and Michigan, inmates without jobs said they were too busy with other activities, or simply did not want a job. Only about 20 percent said that jobs were unavailable. In Texas, about 25 percent said jobs were unavailable, and a greater percentage said they lost their jobs as a result of punishment. These figures raise interesting questions about the relatively low job assignments for blacks in Texas—especially in light of the high value that minorities placed on jobs in all three states. Nevertheless, we found no racial differences in any of the states in the reasons inmates gave for not having a prison job.

Although their primary purpose is maintenance of the institution, prison work assignments seem to be providing skills that the inmates believe will help them gain employment upon release. About one-third of the inmates with prison jobs thought they would provide "a lot" of help to them in terms of future employment. This is a rather large fraction, considering that only 66 percent of the inmates enrolled in vocational training programs judged them to be "a lot" of help in terms of future employment.

Across all three states, more minority inmates than whites rated their job assignments as helpful to them.

When the three states were compared, programs in Michigan and Texas were judged as more helpful than those in California. The percentages of those who rated their work assignments as "no help" were 51 percent in California, 45 percent in Texas, and only 34 percent in Michigan.

Conclusions Concerning In-Prison Programs and Work Assignments

We found few racial differences in program participation or work assignments among prison inmates in our sample. Where we found differences, they seemed to result from inmates' priorities and attitudes instead of from prison staff decisions.

Among programs, there was a closer match between need and participation in educational and vocational training than in drug and alcohol rehabilitation programs. Evidently, the desire to become more employable on the outside motivated prisoners more strongly than the objectives of the other rehabilitation programs we studied. Across states and races, we found that many prisoners with high need for alcohol and drug rehabilitation who did not participate generally claimed that they did not need help with their problems. This was especially true of blacks and alcohol programs. Even though they had a much lower need for alcohol rehabilitation than whites or Hispanics, a much lower proportion of blacks with need participated in alcohol programs. However, our examination of motives for failure to participate indicates that, if there was discrimination here, the black inmates were discriminating against the program, not vice versa. For drug rehabilitation programs, there was evidence that, in some prisons, programs were not available where prisoners with high need would have participated, but there was no suggestion of racial differences.

The picture for jobs was similar. Although a lower proportion of blacks had jobs in Michigan and Texas, inmates without jobs generally said that they were too busy, did not want jobs, or could not have jobs for other reasons. However, there were some interesting coincidences here that might bear investigating. In Texas, where blacks were significantly less likely than whites to have jobs, a high proportion of inmates said they did not work because jobs were unavailable or because of punishment. Further, Texas was also the state in which a smaller proportion of blacks with high need for education were in education programs. These coincidences could represent a pattern that implies discrimination.

Be that as it may, we found no statistically significant racial differences in participation—in proportion of participants who had need, or in job assignments—that necessarily indicate discrimination. That picture changes when we look at length of sentence served.

RACIAL DIFFERENCES IN LENGTH OF SENTENCE SERVED

The final and perhaps most important test of discrimination is whether minorities serve longer in prison than their white counterparts. The National Minority Advisory Council (1980, p. 243) recently concluded:

> The inequity of minority imprisonment is not only one of greater numbers, it is also one of greater duration of confinement once imprisoned. It has become increasingly evident that, proportionally, minority group members convicted of crimes are at greater risk of being: (a) sentenced to a term of imprisonment, (b) sentenced to a longer term of imprisonment, and (c) forced to serve a longer portion of any given term of imprisonment.

Those who argue that minorities serve longer prison sentences usually offer as "evidence" a comparison of the average length of sentence served by members of the different races.

As a measure of discrimination, however, average length of time served is meaningless because the races may differ on other factors that legitimately affect length of term. If a group of black offenders receives or serves longer sentences than a group of whites, we cannot conclude that the difference is due to race alone, unless the two groups are alike in all other respects that legitimately affect sentences. The critical question here is: When we statistically account for the effect of key factors relating to the nature of the offender and the offense, do we find that minorities end up serving longer sentences than similar white offenders?

Length of sentence served is obviously related to the court-imposed sentence, and, as we saw, minorities received longer sentences in all three states. However, it can also be profoundly affected by in-prison behavior. If an offender is well behaved—has a good attitude, participates in treatment, etc.—his sentence can be significantly reduced, either as a result of being awarded good-time credits or being discharged at his earliest parole hearing. The inmates in our sample certainly believed in these effects: Most of them gave "help me get parole" as an important reason for participating in treatment programs.

Nature of Our Analysis

We investigated racial differences in length of sentence served by comparing the average number of months served, while controlling for other related factors. For each inmate who completed our Inmate Survey, we calculated the expected length of sentence in months.[4]

In California, the majority of inmates had originally been sentenced to prison when California's Indeterminate Sentencing Law was in effect. When Determinate Sentencing was adopted in 1977, the California Board of Prison Terms reviewed each inmate's case and computed a new sentence length based on the expected sentence he would have received if he had been sentenced under Determinate Sentencing. Each inmate was then informed of his expected release date. The actual time served will be very close to this number of months, since the expected sentence can only be altered slightly as a result of prison behavior in California. This recomputed sentence length is the number we used for length of sentence served. Unfortunately for analytic purposes, it combines aspects of both indeterminate and determinate sentencing.

For Texas and Michigan, the expected sentence length reflects the inmate's knowledge about when he will get out. In some instances, the sentence will be extended because of disciplinary problems. Estimates made by inmates who are nearing the end of their sentence are undoubtedly more accurate. However, officials in both Texas and Michigan evidently follow a policy of letting inmates know the actual time they will be required to serve as near to the beginning of their terms as possible. Moreover, in these states, terms are usually extended significantly only for major violations, because extreme overcrowd-

---

[4]Expected sentence length was calculated by taking the respondents' answers to "how long have you been here" and "how much longer do you have left to serve" and adding the two numbers together. In addition, these numbers were compared with the expected "date of release" supplied by the correction departments in each state. The two estimates were very closely correlated (see Marquis and Ebener, 1981).

ing in prisons makes extension for minor violations impractical. Our data show that less than 10 percent of the inmates in these states commit serious infractions during their terms. Consequently, few inmates will have their imposed sentence significantly extended.

To discover whether these sentence lengths varied for whites and minorities, when other relevant factors were controlled, we began with a cross-tabular analysis. Because sentences served differ significantly for the states, we had to examine racial differences for each state separately.[5]

In this analysis, we controlled for state, race, conviction type, and prior record. The results are shown in Table 5.1.

There are selected instances, particularly in Texas and California, where minorities appear to be serving longer terms, but they do not reach statistical significance. For example, in Texas, blacks with no prior prison record serve an average of 50 months for robbery, whereas whites serve 37 months. Blacks with a prior prison record serve 87 months for robbery, whereas whites serve 67 months. Hispanics appear to be serving longer terms in California, especially when compared with whites. In the case of robbery, for example, Hispanics with no prior prison record serve an average of 47 months compared with 44 months for whites. Hispanics with a prior prison record serve 54 months for robbery, compared with 47 for whites and 40 for blacks. For most crimes and prior record categories, Hispanics in California appear to serve longer terms than either whites or blacks. However, there are no obvious racial differences in Michigan. Moreover, this analysis yielded few statistically significant differences of any kind.

This cross-tabular approach has limitations. As more stratifications are introduced, the resulting tables have more and more cells; the number of inmates falling in each cell becomes smaller; the racial differences within each cell become more and more unstable; and it becomes difficult to estimate some "overall" racial differences. To overcome these limitations and see if there were any statistically significant racial differences in sentence served, we again turned to the multivariate regression technique. This was the technique we used in analyzing racial differences in court-imposed sentences, reported in Sec. III. This technique permitted us to control for all of the following independent variables:

---

[5]California inmates served less time for most crime types than inmates in either Texas or Michigan. For example, Texas and Michigan inmates served about 55 months for robbery and 40 for burglary, while California inmates served almost 10 months less on the average—46 months for robbery and 25 for burglary.

Table 5.1

TIME SERVED BY CONVICTION OFFENSE, RACE, AND PRIOR RECORD

(In months)

Prior Record	California				Michigan				Texas			
	White	Black	Hispanic	Chi-Square	White	Black	Hispanic	Chi-Square	White	Black	Hispanic	Chi-Square
Homicide												
No prior prison	47	59	55	NS	85	89	--	NS	49	71	70	NS
1 or more prior prison	56	77	62	NS	125	77	--	<.05	48	102	34	NS
Serious personal crime[a]												
No prior prison	41	46	45	NS	37	53	--	<.05	32	48	78	NS
1 or more prior prison	46	59	66	NS	75	53	--	NS	83	68	34	NS
Robbery												
No prior prison	44	42	47	NS	47	58	--	NS	37	50	45	<.01
1 or more prior prison	47	40	54	NS	42	62	--	<.10	67	87	90	NS
Property crime												
No prior prison	23	21	28	NS	33	36	--	NS	32	32	42	NS
1 prior prison	22	21	25	NS	33	27	--	NS	36	40	31	NS
2 or more prior prison	26	30	34	NS	46	47	--	NS	61	60	88	NS
Miscellaneous												
No prior prison	37	16	13	NS	38	41	--	NS	41	21	18	NS
1 prior prison	27	15	--	NS	55	30	--	NS	38	76	29	NS

[a] Serious personal crimes include rape, kidnapping, and aggravated assault.

Legal Factors

Current conviction crime type
Number of previous juvenile and adult incarcerations

Personal and Biographic Factors

Age	Drug use
Education	Alcohol use
Marital status	Employment history
Race	Psychiatric history

In-Prison Factors

Extent and type of infractions in current prison term
Extent of participation in prison treatment and work programs during current term
Time spent in disciplinary segregation during current term

Findings

Results for California. Our regression analysis showed that length of sentence served in California was significantly related to age, offense type, race, prison infractions, and marital status (see App. C). The estimates of their effects are given in Table 5.2. The table indicates that in California:

- Blacks serve 2.4 months longer than whites.
- Hispanics serve five months longer than whites.
- These differences are not due to age, offense, infractions, or marital differences among the races.

Results for Texas. In Texas, we discovered that sentence length is related primarily to age, offense type, race, time spent in segregation, and prior record. The results are summarized in Table 5.3.

The racial effect is stronger in Texas than in California. We find:

- Blacks serve sentences that are 7.7 months longer than those served by whites.
- Hispanics serve sentences that are 8.1 months longer than those served by whites.
- These differences are not due to age, offense, prior record, or behavior while in prison, and they are not fully accounted for by length of sentence originally imposed.

Table 5.2

CALIFORNIA SENTENCE-LENGTH SERVED MODEL

Item	Sentence Length Served
Basic Sentence[a]	44.0 months
Age adjustment	
Under 22 years old	4.4 months lower
23-26 years	0.3 months lower
27-31 years	1.8 months higher
Over 32 years	2.9 months higher
Offense adjustment	
Homicide	12.5 months higher
Personal violence	4.5 months higher
Robbery	1.4 months higher
Property	18.4 months lower
Race adjustment	
Whites	2.5 months lower
Blacks	0.1 months lower
Hispanics	2.5 months higher
Other	
One or more infractions	4.2 months higher
Not married	4.5 months lower

[a]The basic sentence is not the same as the average sentence; rather, it is what the average would have been if each of the factors in the model had divided the population into equal numbers.

Results for Michigan. In Michigan, we discovered that time served depended primarily on age, offense type, juvenile record, and time spent in segregation. Race had no statistically significant effect on sentence length served, although blacks served an average of 1.7 months longer than whites. (See Table 5.4.)

CONCLUSIONS

The criminal justice system evidently treats minorities no differently from whites in allocating correctional services. Although we saw

Table 5.3

TEXAS SENTENCE-LENGTH SERVED MODEL

Item	Sentence Length Served
Basic sentence	48.0
Age adjustment	
Under 22 years	10.2 months lower
23-26 years	7.9 months lower
27-31 years	4.7 months higher
Over 32 years	13.3 months higher
Offense adjustment	
Homicide	9.4 months higher
Personal violence	1.3 months lower
Robbery	2.7 months higher
Property	11.0 months lower
Race adjustment	
Whites	5.3 months lower
Blacks	2.4 months higher
Hispanics	2.8 months higher
Other	
Spent time in hole	10.4 months higher
At least one prior prison term	8.9 months higher

some racial differences in program participation and work assignment, most of these differences were not statistically significant and did not imply discrimination on the part of prison staff or guards. If prisoners want to participate in programs or want to work, the survey indicates that they usually can. When they cannot, the reason seems to be that the programs (e.g., drug rehabilitation) or jobs are not available. There are some provocative patterns in Texas, but even there, black inmates did not say that their failure to participate in, for example, education programs resulted primarily from staff discouragement. All in all, corrections in our sample states evidence no significant racial differences in allocating treatment services to inmates.

The same cannot be said for length of sentence imposed or ultimately served. The results in Sec. III indicated that in California, Texas,

Table 5.4

MICHIGAN SENTENCE-LENGTH SERVED MODEL

Item	Sentence Length Served	
Basic sentence	38.5 months	
Age adjustment		
Under 22 years old	1.8 months	higher
23-26 years	4.8 months	lower
27-31 years	3.3 months	higher
Over 32 years	0.2 months	lower
Offense adjustment		
Homicide	24.2 months	higher
Personal violence	5.5 months	lower
Robbery	1.5 months	lower
Property	17.2 months	lower
Other		
Spent time in hole	2.8 months	higher
Was in state juvenile facility	5.3 months	higher
Was in maximum security	27.5 months	higher

and Michigan, with other relevant factors held equal, minorities *received* longer sentences than whites. In analyzing time served, we found that they also *served* longer sentences, but not significantly so in Michigan. Table 5.5 summarizes the figures for minority sentences received and served—relative to sentences for whites—in the three states.

Although we discuss the larger implications of these differences in the final section, some discussion of their possible cause seems appropriate here. One explanation may be that these states have different sentencing/parole structures.

California has a Determinate Sentencing Law, and there is no active parole board, except for life-termers. Although inmates may earn good-time credits for good behavior and program participation, these credits actually reduce sentences very little. Consequently, time served reflects sentence imposed fairly closely, and racial disparities in the former result from sentencing decisions. As Table 5.5 shows, these disparities are greater for Hispanics.

Table 5.5

SENTENCES FOR MINORITIES RELATIVE TO THOSE
FOR WHITES

State and Race	Court-Imposed Sentence	Length of Sentence Served
California		
Blacks	+1.4 months	+2.4 months*
Hispanics	+6.5 months*	+5.0 months*
Michigan		
Blacks	+7.2 months*	1.7 months
Hispanics	(small sample)	(small sample)
Texas		
Blacks	+3.7 months	+7.7 months*
Hispanics	+2.0 months	+8.1 months*

*Statistically significant

Texas has indeterminate sentencing and a very active parole board. Time ultimately served is considerably affected by the parole board's decision and the inmate's ability to earn good-time credits.[6] Prison administrators suggest that the Texas board tries to make the parole process as individual as possible, taking into consideration socioeconomic factors as well as legal indicators of personal culpability. These factors evidently work to the relative advantage of white inmates, to the disadvantage of minority inmates, or both. As Table 5.5 indicates, the gap between sentence imposed and sentence served widens for minorities in Texas prisons.

Michigan has a modified indeterminate sentencing policy and a very active parole board. In 1976, it began using a risk assessment scheme in making many of its parole decisions. The scheme primarily uses three personal indicators of culpability: juvenile criminal history, conviction crime, and prison behavior. This system has dramatically affected parole decisions; it partly reflects the parole board's

---

[6]Because good-time credits are awarded on a graduated scale, Texas inmates can actually earn a day off their sentences for every day served, once they reach a certain point on the scale. In contrast, at the time of our study, California did not apportion credits that generously.

desire to see that offenders convicted for similar crimes should serve roughly equal time in prison. As Table 5.5 suggests, this attitude and the risk-assessment system appear to have overcome racial disparities in court-imposed sentences for blacks. The regression analyses show that even though blacks are sentenced to 7.2 months more than whites, they serve roughly the same time. Commendable as the effort to overcome racial disparities in time served may be, it may not necessarily accord with the parole board's central mandate—to assess the risk that a criminal presents to society when he leaves prison. This is a dilemma we discuss further in the last section.

With the exception of crime commission rates and program participation, we have been looking so far at racial differences in the system's treatment of offenders rather than possible racial differences in behavior that might influence that treatment. In defending the system against charges of discrimination, some people have argued that the racial differences in treatment result from racial differences in behavior. To assess that argument, the next section looks at the motivation for crime, use of weapons, and in-prison violence in our sample.

VI. RACIAL DIFFERENCES IN CRIME MOTIVATIONS, WEAPONS USE, AND PRISON INFRACTIONS

It seems obvious that numerous aspects of an offender's behavior will influence the impression he makes on probation officers, judges, and parole boards. Section V indicated that infractions of prison rules and punishment suffered for those infractions were related to sentence served in two states. Added to the effects of race in California, for example, such infractions could result in black prisoners serving even longer terms. We believe that behavior, such as crime motivation and weapon use, might have a similar effect on sentencing. If there are *racial* differences in these kinds of behavior, they might help account for some of the racial differences we saw in sentencing and length of sentence served.

CRIME MOTIVATIONS

To explore crime motivations, we asked survey respondents to rate how important the potential reasons shown in Table 6.1 were for the crimes they had committed during the window period (the 12 to 24 months immediately preceding their current imprisonment). They rated them on a four-point scale from very important (scale score = 4) to not important at all (scale score = 1). In our motivational analysis, we combined the three states' results because preliminary analysis showed no significant differences in motivations among the states. We also combined the categories "somewhat" and "slightly" important, and the categories "not important" and "did not apply."

Our motivational question and our analysis plan are patterned after work done by Peterson and Braiker (1981). They posed a similar question to inmates in a survey conducted in 1976. Their sample included only California, was smaller than ours, and was for a period two years earlier. Nevertheless, their results and ours are almost identical: The percent of their sample who rated specific reasons as "very important" is, in most instances, within 5 percent of that in our sample. The compatibility of the two studies lends credibility to this question, as well as confidence that it is in fact measuring rather consistently the array of reasons inmates have for engaging in crime.

Table 6.1

SELF-REPORTED REASONS FOR COMMITTING CRIMES, THREE STATES COMBINED

(In percent)

Reason[a]	Very Important	Somewhat/ Slightly Important	Not Important at All
Losing your job	22	23	55
Heavy debts	13	22	65
Good opportunity	14	40	46
Couldn't get a job	23	23	54
Revenge or anger	7	16	76
Excitement and kicks	5	23	71
To get money for good times and high living	18	39	43
Friends' ideas	4	25	71
To get money for drugs	20	21	58
To get money for rent, food, self-support	39	27	34
Just felt nervous and tense	4	17	80
Blew up--lost your cool	8	18	74
Because you had taken drugs	11	19	70
Because you had been drinking	11	19	70

[a]Respondents rated the importance of each listed reason in response to the following question: "This is a list of reasons men have given for doing crimes. Go through the whole list and show how important each reason was for the crimes you did during the STREET MONTHS ON THE CALENDAR. (Circle a number for each reason.)"

Results for All Inmates

The results in Table 6.1 indicate that more than half the respondents rated "to get money for rent, food, and self-support," "good opportunity," and "to get money for good times and high living" as either very important or somewhat/slightly important reasons. For a substantial number, drugs and unemployment appeared to be important motivations. Slightly less than half of the sample described "losing your job" (45 percent), "couldn't get a job" (46 percent), or "to get money for drugs" (41 percent) as very or somewhat/slightly important. "Because you had taken drugs" or "because you had been drinking" were important to 30 percent of the respondents. In contrast, about three-quarters of the respondents did not regard temper, tension, or the influence of others as important reasons for their crimes.

Racial Differences in Crime Motivation

Table 6.2 shows the percentage of each racial group who rated a motivation as "very important." There are statistically significant racial differences in several items. A greater percentage of black respondents reported that "losing their job," "being unable to get a job," or "needing money for self-support" was very important. White offenders were more likely to report that having taken drugs or alcohol was very important to their crimes, as well as the need to get money for drugs.

Table 6.2

FACTORS RATED AS VERY IMPORTANT CRIME MOTIVATIONS, BY RACE;
THREE STATES COMBINED

(In percent)

Reason	White	Black	Hispanic	Chi-Square[a]	Total
Losing your job	17	27	20	<.001	22
Heavy debts	11	15	10	<.001	13
Good opportunity	15	13	11	<.001	14
Couldn't get a job	20	26	15	<.05	23
Revenge or anger	8	7	4	<.05	7
Excitement and kicks	9	4	1	<.001	5
To get money for good times and high living	18	19	15	NS	18
Friends' ideas	5	4	3	NS	4
To get money for drugs	25	16	24	<.001	20
To get money for rent, food, self-support	37	41	33	NS	39
Just felt nervous and tense	4	4	2	NS	4
Blew up--lost your cool	9	8	6	NS	8
Because you had taken drugs	15	8	14	<.001	11
Because you had been drinking	16	7	15	<.001	11

[a]The chi-square test was performed using all of the ratings together. Only ratings of "very important" are reproduced here.

To explore the dimensions of motivation, Peterson and Braiker conducted a factor analysis on their samples' responses that yielded three orthogonal factors, i.e., groups of items that were statistically unrelated to each other: economic distress, "high times," and temper. Because our preliminary analysis showed identical results, we adopted their scales for our use. Table 6.3 shows the three orthogonal factors and the items that loaded on each.[1]

The entire sample and each racial group rated the reasons under "economic distress" as the most important to their crimes. The score was highest for blacks, but this racial difference was not statistically significant. We must be cautious about these results, however. Many inmates may have seized on economic distress as a plausible excuse for their crimes. Nevertheless, by the study's own need criteria, a very high percentage of the inmates were identified as needing vocational training—blacks most of all, in the three states—and the criteria derived primarily from employment history (see Fig. 5.3).

The "high times" factor embodies hedonistic reasons for crime: excitement and "kicks," the influence of drugs or alcohol, or the challenge of a good opportunity. These reasons were rated as less important than economic distress, but more important than temper. White offenders scored higher on this scale.

The "temper" scale yielded no racial differences.

Although most of these findings revealed no statistically significant racial differences, they raise some provocative questions. Blacks rated economic distress considerably higher than high times, while whites rated economic distress only slightly higher. The suggestion is that socioeconomic conditions among blacks may be more consistent and more consistently related to crime than they are among whites. Certainly, that comes as no particular surprise; but if probation officers, judges, and parole boards see past unemployment as an indicator of recidivism—rather than as a mitigating circumstance in crime—blacks or any other unemployed offenders are likely to receive harsher sentences. We discuss the effects of recidivism indicators on sentencing and time served in the last section.

RACIAL DIFFERENCES IN WEAPON USE AND VICTIM INJURY

The type of weapon an offender uses and the frequency with which he uses it are important dimensions of his criminal behavior. They indicate in some measure his commitment to a criminal life-style, his

---

[1]In our analysis, friends' ideas did not clearly load on any single factor. This was also true with the Peterson and Braiker analysis.

Table 6.3

IMPORTANCE OF MOTIVATION SCALES, BY RACE

Motivation Scale Name[a]	Reasons Included in Scale[b]	Importance of Scale[c]				
		White	Black	Hispanic	Chi-Square[d]	Overall
Economic distress[e]	Losing your job Heavy debts Couldn't get a job To get money for rent, food, self-support	1.69	1.75	1.63	NS	1.71
High times[f]	To get money for good times and high living Excitement and kicks To get money for drugs Because of drugs Because of alcohol Good opportunity	1.63	1.45	1.55	<.001	1.52
Temper[g]	Revenge or anger Blew up--lost my cool Just felt nervous and tense	1.33	1.27	1.26	NS	1.29

[a]Derived from principal components factor analysis, 3-factor verimax rotated solution.

[b]Listed in order of magnitude of factor loadings.

[c]Higher scores indicate that scale was more important to respondents. Scores indicate mean importance rating across items for each motivation scale based on 3-point Likert scale (3 = very important, 2 = somewhat/slightly important, 1 = not important at all).

[d]Used the Kruskal-Wallis Test (chi-square to approximation) to test differences between the ranks.

[e]Reliability = .73, N=1092. Scale scores were calculated using data from respondents who answered at least three of the Economic Distress items. Theta reliability coefficient calculated as $(*h = p (p - 1) (*1 - 1)(*1)$, where p = number of items in the factor scale and $(*1)$ = latent root from principal components analysis.

[f]Reliability = .65, N = 1072. Scale scores were calculated using data from respondents who answered at least four of the High Times items.

[g]Reliability = .68, N = 1084. Scale scores were calculated using data from respondents who answered at least two of the Temper items.

professionalism, and his attitude toward legal penalties for using weapons. Weapon use also says something about his motives and the context in which he anticipates committing his crimes (e.g., premeditated vs. impulsive).

These implied attitudes might be expected to affect the offender's sentence and time served. As we conjectured in looking at motivations, if there are racial differences in the kind and degree of weapon use, they might help explain racial differences in treatment. For that reason, the Inmate Survey asked each inmate who reported committing one or more crimes of burglary, robbery, or assault during the study period a series of questions concerning weapon use and victim injury.[2]

Weapon Use for Particular Crimes. Table 6.4 shows the results. In kind and degree of weapon use, business and personal robbery are very different from burglary. Robberies involve more weapons, with firearms predominating, and business robberies are seldom committed without a formidable weapon. It is also possible that older, more sophisticated offenders, tend to favor robbery—particularly commercial robbery—more than do younger, unsophisticated offenders. The patterns for aggravated assault are very similar to those for personal robberies.

Table 6.5 examines whether there are racial differences in the percentages who report that they were usually armed with a weapon (either "always" or "half or more" of the time) in their crimes. Few racial differences appear in the overall extent of weapon use. However, there is a suggestive trend, which reaches statistical significance only for burglary, in which Hispanics were those most likely to carry a weapon of some sort.

We found no statistically significant racial differences in gun use, but it is interesting to note that Hispanics were the least likely to use a gun, particularly in the two types of robbery. Among white offenders, 71 percent were "always" armed with a gun during a business robbery, whereas this was true for only 64 percent of the blacks and 51 percent of the Hispanics. The trends were similar for burglary and personal robbery.

Significant racial differences appeared in the frequency of knife use. For each of the four study crimes, Hispanics most often reported being armed with knives (statistically significant for each of the crime types). Blacks reported a very low incidence of knife use, especially in burglary and business robbery.

The analysis of the extent and type of weapons used revealed racial differences: Hispanics show a preference for knives; whites show a

---

[2]See Chaiken and Chaiken (1982) for exact questions asked.

Table 6.4

TYPE OF WEAPON USUALLY USED IN COMMITTING CRIME
(Percent of Those Committing the Crime; Three States Combined)

Type of Weapon Used	Crime Type			
	Burglary	Business Robbery	Personal Robbery	Aggravated Assault
Knife	13	7	16	27
Firearm	27	80	64	55
Other	0	0.9	0.7	2
None	60	12	19	16

Table 6.5

PERCENT USUALLY CARRYING WEAPONS DURING CRIMES[a]
(Weapon Types Combined; Three States Combined)

Race	Burglary	Business Robbery	Personal Robbery	Assault
White	47	88	83	80
Black	31	86	79	86
Hispanic	51	94	85	86
All races combined	40	88	81	83
Chi-square	<.001	NS	NS	NS

[a]Calculated as percent of those who reported committing at least one of that type of crime during the window period.

clear preference for guns; blacks show a preference for guns but not to the extent that whites do. However, when we *combine* all weapon types and look at the percentages of those who were armed at all during a crime, only one significant difference appears: Blacks are less likely to be armed during burglary.

Extent of Victim Injury. Respondents who reported committing at least one crime of robbery, burglary, or assault during the study period were asked a series of questions pertaining to any victim injuries. We found no statistically significant racial differences in the percentage of offenders who reported seriously—"perhaps" fatally—injuring their victims.[3] Again, however, some interesting and consistent trends appeared. In the assault category, a greater proportion of Hispanics reported both seriously injuring their victims (82 percent as opposed to 73 percent for whites and 69 percent for blacks) and the possibility that death might have resulted (27 percent for Hispanics, 20 percent for blacks, and 19 percent for whites). We found no differences for robbery or burglary, however. Of the inmates who reported assaulting their victims during those crimes, 65 to 70 percent reported that the victim's injuries were serious, and 25 to 35 percent thought their victims might have died.

Our findings suggest, then, that there are racial "preferences" for particular weapons and that some groups are more likely than others to be armed during some types of crimes. That evidence is certainly not strong enough to suggest it may be an important factor contributing to differences in sentencing or parole decisions, but it permits some conjectures. Hispanics are more likely than whites to be sent to prison and stay there longer, and Hispanics show a statistically significant preference for using knives—in all crimes. Moreover, their responses indicate a much greater tendency to seriously injure their victims. If this is evidence of a propensity to violence, and if that propensity manifests itself in demeanor or manner during court or parole hearings, these factors might influence sentencing and parole.

Provocative as these conjectures may be, the statistics for blacks suggest the opposite. As Fig. 1.2 has indicated, the proportion of blacks in prison for burglary was considerably higher than the proportion of blacks arrested for burglary. Yet, blacks in our sample were significantly less likely to be armed during burglaries. Indeed, they were less likely than whites to use guns and less likely than Hispanics to use knives. Does this indicate that they are less violent criminals than either group and, perhaps, less "professional"? If so, probation officers, judges, and parole boards apparently do not recog-

---

[3]Our questionnaire avoided asking directly about murder since the validity of the responses might have been questionable, given the sensitive nature of the subject. Instead, we asked whether they thought their victim "might have died."

nize these as mitigating characteristics. Our findings on prison violence raise similarly conflicting suggestions.

RACIAL DIFFERENCES IN PRISON VIOLENCE

Despite a wide variation in research methodologies, a synthesis of the literature on prison behavior indicates that inmates involved in disciplinary problems tend to be young, to have juvenile arrest records, and to have started their criminal careers at an early age.[4] There is no clear trend in the literature regarding the relationship between prison violence and race, type of commitment offense, and prior prison terms.

Institutional infractions provided our measure of prison behavior. Using that measure, we analyzed behavior of the different races by examining the effect that each component variable has on prison behavior. The analysis included such inmate characteristics as age, race, prior record, and commitment offense, and such in-prison variables as months in prison, prison work status, and level of participation in treatment programs.

Table 6.6 lists, in order of increasing severity, the seven types of infractions we used to code disciplinary reports. Each inmate's folder contains a copy of all the disciplinary reports he received during his current term; we recorded their numbers and types. Although the typical infraction fit more than one category (e.g., an inmate threatened and seriously injured another inmate with a contraband weapon), for simplicity we recorded only the most serious infraction (e.g., major injury).

Differences in Prison Violence Among States

Table 6.7 shows the percentages of inmates in each state who had at least one officially recorded infraction. The percentages vary across states and differ significantly for five of the seven infraction types studied. Of those five, Michigan inmates had a much higher percentage than Texas or California inmates, except for infractions involving contraband. The percentage of Texas inmates with at least one infraction is less than one-third that of Michigan or California inmates. A greater percentage of Michigan inmates have at least one "write-up"

---

[4]See, for example, Myers and Levy (1978); Ellis et al. (1974); Bolte (1978); Brown and Spevacek (1969); Jaman (1972); Bennett (1976); Flanagan (1980, 1983); Coe (1961); and Fuller and Orsagh (1977).

Table 6.6

Types and Descriptions of Infractions

Infraction Type	Description
Administrative	Disobedience, gambling, theft, horseplay, out-of-place, noncoercive homosexuality, work-related and other nonserious charges.
Contraband	Concealment or possession of items in violation of rules (e.g., drugs, weapons, literature).
Threat	Statement or gesture indicating intent to harm, coerce, intimidate, etc.
Violence without injury	Destruction of state property, fight or assault not resulting in an injury (but more serious than horseplay).
Minor injury	Fight or assault resulting in cut, bruise, needing only slight medical treatment.
Major injury	Fight or assault resulting in injury requiring medical treatment or observation.
Escape	Plots, attempts, conspiracies.

for each infraction type except major injury. We found that the total number of infractions also varied considerably across states. Only 30 percent of the Michigan inmates had no infractions compared with 41 percent of the California and 46 percent of Texas inmates.

We are at present unable to determine how much of the variation in state infraction rates is attributable to inmate behavior and how much to differing state policies.[5] The variation led us to analyze racial differences in prison violence state by state.

---

[5]Although these findings suggest that the level of negative inmate behavior is higher in Michigan than in California or Texas, we believe these differences can be explained in part by the disciplinary policies and procedures in the three states. In our opinion, the Michigan data probably reflect more accurately the actual level of inmate behavior problems. In California prisons, where staff members perceive a greater potential for more serious inmate disturbances, minor transgressions are often ignored as a tradeoff for continued order in prison. In Texas, the omnipresent threat of losing good-time credits and being returned to the fields to do agricultural labor ("to the line") tends to hold down the number of inmate transgressions. Also, Texas prison officials spoke of informal procedures (short of writing a disciplinary report) for handling some minor infractions.

Table 6.7

PERCENT OF INMATES WITH INFRACTIONS, BY STATE AND
TYPE OF INFRACTION

Infraction Type	California (N=337)	Michigan (N=363)	Texas (N=583)	Chi-Square
Administrative	44.7	60.1	47.5	<.05
Contraband	24.3	29.8	7:9	<.05
Threat	4.2	13.8	1.2	<.05
Violence without injury	15.1	27.5	18.0	<.05
Minor injury	1.5	5.0	1.4	NS
Major injury	3.3	1.4	0.9	NS
Escape	1.2	8.0	0.3	<.05

Racial Differences in Prison Violence

Table 6.8 tabulates infractions by race. In California, the only significant racial difference is that whites had the greatest incidence of contraband infractions (31 percent), followed by Hispanics (15 percent) and then blacks (15 percent). Racial differences for other infractions did not reach statistical significance, although there was a definite trend, with whites having a greater frequency of most infraction types, the only exception being major injury (where Hispanics have the greatest number).

The opposite situation exists in Michigan: Percentagewise, blacks have the most infractions classified as administrative, threat, and violence involving both major and minor injuries.

Texas resembles Michigan in that a greater percentage of the minority population (both blacks and Hispanics) has at least one infraction for each type—but there are significant differences between the races for administrative infractions and violence without injury only.

The analysis represented in Table 6.8 does not take into account the actual number of infractions or how long an inmate has been in prison. An inmate with several infractions over a few months is clearly more troublesome than one who has the same number of infractions but has been in prison several years. Nor does it control for other factors that may be related to prison violence (e.g., age). To account for their effects, we again used a multiple regression model, applied separately to each state.

Table 6.8

PERCENT OF INMATES WHO HAVE AT LEAST ONE INFRACTION, BY TYPE AND RACE

Infraction Type	California				Michigan				Texas			
	White	Black	Hispanic	Chi-Square	White	Black	Hispanic	Chi-Square	White	Black	Hispanic	Chi-Square
Administrative	42	38	37	NS	51	65	50	<.05	28	40	36	<.05
Contraband	31	15	25	<.05	27	30	50	NS	8	8	13	NS
Threat	5	6	0	NS	12	14	0	NS	1	1	0	NS
Violence without injury	8	4	3	NS	20	32	30	NS	8	26	15	<.001
Minor injury[a]	3	0	0	<.05	1	7	0	<.05	2	2	0	NS
Major injury[a]	3	3	5	NS	1	2	0	NS	0	2	0	NS
Escape[a]	2	1	0	NS	10	7	20	NS	0	0	2	NS

[a]In some instances, these categories have expected counts of less than 5. Because of the small cell sizes, the chi-square might not be a valid test.

The Relation of Race and Other Factors to Prison Violence

For the regression analysis, we wanted our dependent variable to reflect both the number and seriousness of infractions. We therefore created a "weighted" infractions score by assigning administrative infractions a weight of 1, and adding a weight of 1 to each increasingly serious type of infraction. The infraction types thus had the following weights: administrative, 1; possession of contraband, 2; threat, 3; violence without injury, 4; minor injury, 5; major injury, 6; and escape, 7. Each inmate's infractions were weighted, then summed, divided by the total number of months he had been in prison, and multiplied by 12 to get an annual rate. This weighted infractions rate is our dependent variable in the regression analysis. Our independent variables reflected both preprison and in-prison factors. They included:

- Age
- Race
- Prior adult and juvenile criminal record
- Current conviction crime
- Age at first arrest
- Having a prison work assignment
- Extent of treatment program participation
- Months served on this sentence

The complete regression results are reproduced in App. D. They show that in California, inmate age is most strongly (negatively) related to infractions. This is consistent with prior research. We also find significant inverse relationships for inmate race, prison work status, and treatment participation rates. Whites (the reference group) have significantly more infractions than blacks (although not substantially more than Hispanics). Further, all other things equal, inmates without prison jobs and with less exposure to treatment programs tend to have significantly higher infraction rates than their counterparts. The "idle" inmate represents the extreme case for these latter variables.

In Michigan, also, inmate age is most strongly (negatively) related to infractions. Further, only one of the four criminal history variables was statistically significant ($p < .01$): Criminals currently convicted of a nonviolent offense had higher infraction rates than those convicted of a violent offense. Unlike the results in California, inmate race was not significantly associated with infractions. Also, neither the degree to which the inmate had participated in treatment programs nor the inmate's prison work status was statistically associated with infractions.

In Texas, as in Michigan and California, there was a powerful (negative) relationship between inmate age and infraction rates. As was the case in California, race was statistically significant in Texas, but in the opposite direction: Black inmates in Texas had a higher infraction rate than whites. And, as in Michigan, only one criminal history variable was significant: the number of prior convictions. Finally, as in California, Texas inmates with greater treatment program participation and prison work assignments had significantly lower rates of infractions than their counterparts.

In sum, the high-rate infractor for each state had the following profile:

- *California:* A young white inmate who has had limited exposure to treatment programs, and who currently has no prison work assignment.
- *Michigan:* A young inmate serving a prison sentence for a nonviolent crime.
- *Texas:* A young black inmate with few serious convictions, who has had limited exposure to treatment programs and who currently has no prison work assignment.

These results show that criminal-history variables were less strongly related to infractions than certain inmate characteristics and in-prison variables. Of the six criminal history variables analyzed, none was significant in California, only one was significant in Michigan (conviction crime type), and only one in Texas (number of serious convictions). We conclude that knowing an inmate's criminal characteristics, other things being equal, does not appreciably increase our predictive capabilities regarding his negative prison behavior.

Of the other independent variables we examined, only inmate age was related to the infractions in all three states: As age increased, the level of infractions decreased. This powerful negative relationship with poor prison behavior confirms prior research.

Our findings on race were also consistent with earlier research; the data reveal mixed results. In Texas, black inmates had significantly higher scores than whites; the reverse was true in California. The sign of the race coefficient in Michigan, although not statistically significant, parallels that of Texas. One possible explanation for these inconsistent results may be different racial compositions in the three prison systems. In Texas and Michigan, blacks constitute the largest racial group; in California, whites are more prevalent. It would seem that the proportion of racial groups in prison is a factor worthy of further investigation in research on negative prison behavior.[6]

---

[6]We find some support for this notion already in the literature. One study of inmate behavior compared prisons where more than half of the inmates were white with pris-

We also found rather strong associations between idleness and infractions. Moreover, improvements in behavior were more related to having a work assignment than to treatment participation, but the best results were achieved by providing both. We make no causal inference here because our data do not permit us to determine whether idle inmates commit more violations than active inmates or whether inmates who commit more violations become idle, i.e., lose their jobs or are removed from a treatment program as punishment.

Unravelling the causality in these relationships is vitally important, especially for examining racial differences in corrections. As we saw in looking at program participation, black inmates in Texas who had high need for education were less likely than whites to be in education programs. They were also less likely to have work assignments in Texas, and it is there that black inmates have a much higher percentage of infractions than whites.

All in all, our results for prison violence are more suggestive than conclusive. Like the findings on criminal motivation and weapon use, they imply that if officials are aware of and responding to these aspects of criminal behavior, they are doing so inconsistently. Blacks serve longer sentences than whites in California and Texas, but only in Texas do they have a higher percentage of infractions. The California and Texas sentencing models both showed that infractions (or punishment of) were related to sentence length served. Yet, the black California inmates' relative lack of infractions evidently does not overcome any of the racial differences in sentence length.

CONCLUSIONS

Although few of the findings are statistically significant, the study shows some racial differences in criminal motivation, weapon use, and prison behavior. However, these differences do little to explain why minorities are more likely than whites to go to prison and stay there longer.

All three groups rated economic distress as their strongest criminal motivation, and whites rated "high times" almost as high. One might expect probation officers, judges, and corrections officials to take a

---

ons where more than half were nonwhite. It found higher average levels of aggressive transgressions, and was able to explain 15 percent more of the variation, in high nonwhite facilities (Ellis et al., 1974). We find similar results despite the differing foci, i.e., state as opposed to institutional differences. Michigan (high black) has a higher average infraction rate than California (low black), although this does not hold true for Texas.

harsher view of "high times" as a motive. However, whites are not sentenced to prison as often or kept there as long. If economic distress is seen as an indicator of recidivism, one would expect prison rehabilitation efforts to focus on vocational training for blacks, who rated economic distress by far their strongest motivation. Yet, as Sec. 5 indicated, blacks were no more likely than whites to participate in vocational training programs.

The findings on weapon use are equally ambiguous. There were few clear trends, but statistically significant racial differences. Hispanics strongly preferred knives and were more likely to report doing grievous harm to their victims. It seems possible that this behavior could legitimately lead to harsher sentences and longer time served. Blacks were much less likely than Hispanics to use a knife, and less likely than whites to use a gun. Indeed, when the study *combined all crime types* and looked at the overall percent of racial groups armed during a crime, there was only one statistically significant difference: Blacks were less likely to be armed in a burglary. Nevertheless, blacks make up a larger percent of the prison than of the arrest population for burglary.

We find very significant racial differences in prison behavior in the study states. Yet, those differences do not coincide with length of sentence served for similar crimes. For example, in California, whites have a significantly higher rate of prison infractions than blacks. In Texas, the reverse is true. Yet in both states, blacks serve longer sentences.

Having looked at the criminal justice system's treatment of offenders and at offenders' behavior, we have still not been able to legitimately account for racial differences in post-arrest release rates, in sentencing, and in length of sentence served. In the next section, we summarize the major findings, draw some conclusions, and look at their implications for future research.

VII. CONCLUSIONS AND IMPLICATIONS OF THE STUDY

For critics of the criminal justice system, the arrest and imprisonment rates for blacks and other minorities suggest that the system discriminates against those groups. They argue, for example, that blacks, who make up 12 percent of the national population, could not possibly commit 48 percent of the crime. Yet that is exactly what arrest and imprisonment rates imply about black criminality. Defenders of the system argue that the arrest and imprisonment rates do not lie; the system simply reacts to the prevalence of crime in the black community. As we have noted repeatedly, prior research has not settled this controversy. For every study that finds discrimination in arrests, convictions, sentencing, prison treatment, or parole, another denies it.

This study has certainly not settled the issue. However, it has overcome the methodological limitations of most previous studies in two ways: (1) by controlling for more variables that may affect treatment of all offenders, and (2) by examining possible racial differences in handling at decision points throughout the system—not at merely one or two points. Further, it has a more comprehensive data base than many other studies because it includes information from both official records and prisoners' self-reports. The results indicate that there are some racial differences in criminal behavior and in the way offenders are treated in the study states. These findings raise important issues for the criminal justice system and suggest priorities for future research.

MAJOR FINDINGS

Before turning to the conclusions and their implications, it is useful to review the major findings. Table 7.1 summarizes particular findings in major categories.

Racial Differences in Case Processing

Although the case processing system generally treated offenders similarly, racial differences appeared at two key points, prefiling release and sentencing. White suspects were less likely than minorities

Table 7.1

SUMMARY OF STUDY FINDINGS

Element Studied	Evidence of Racial Differences[a]
Offender Behavior	
Preference for different crime types	+
Volume of crime committed	0
Crime motivation	++
Type of weapon preferred and extent of its use	++
Victim injury	+
Need for drug and alcohol treatment	0
Need for vocational training and education	+
Assessments of prison program effects	0
Arrest	
Probability of suffering arrest	0
Whether arrested on warrant or probable cause*	+
Probability of having case forwarded to prosecutor*	+
Prosecution and Sentencing	
Whether case is officially filed*	+
Type of charges filed*	0
Reasons for nonprosecution*	+
Whether the case is settled by plea bargaining*	+
Probability of conviction*	0
Type of crime convicted of*	0
Type of sentence imposed*	++
Length of sentence imposed	+
Corrections	
Type of programs participated in	0
Reasons for not participating in programs	0
Probability of having a work assignment	0
Length of sentence served	++
Extent and type of prison infractions	++

SOURCES: The OBTS for starred (*) items; the RIS for all others.

[a] 0 = none; + = suggestive trend; ++ = statistically significant.

to be released after arrest. However, minority offenders convicted of felonies were more likely than whites to go to prison, instead of jail. The findings for misdemeanor convictions were similar: Minorities were more likely to receive sentences instead of probation. If they were sentenced to prison, they also received longer sentences.

Racial Differences in Post-Sentencing Treatment

Post-sentencing treatment shows a racially related inconsistency. In considering participation in treatment and work programs and the reasons inmates gave for not participating, we found no statistically significant differences that implied discrimination against minorities in corrections. However, we found appreciable racial differences in length of sentence served. In California and Texas, when other major factors that might affect release decisions were controlled for, blacks and Hispanics consistently served longer than whites, and the disparity was even greater than the disparity in sentences imposed. In California, blacks served slightly longer sentences, but the disparity largely reflected regional sentencing differences. In Michigan, corrections and parole decisions evidently worked in favor of blacks. Although they initially received sentences considerably longer than those of whites, we found no racial differences in length of time served.

Racial Differences in Crime Commission Rates and Probability of Arrest

The high post-release rates for minorities do not indicate that police overarrest minorities *in proportion to the kind and amount of crime they actually commit*. Our analysis of the Inmate Survey data found that although different racial groups are more likely to commit particular crime types, there are no significant racial differences in crime commission *rates*. Annualized crime commission rates among white and minority criminals are about the same. Moreover, there are no consistent, statistically significant, racial differences in the probability of being arrested, given that a crime has been committed.

Racial Differences in Offender Behavior

There are some clear racial differences in criminal motivation, weapon use, and prison behavior, but most of them do not reach statistical significance. Blacks rated economic distress higher than other motivations for crime, but not significantly more so than other groups. Whites rated hedonistic motives significantly higher than did blacks or Hispanics. In weapons use, there were only two significant findings. Hispanics were much more likely than the other groups to use knives, and blacks were much less likely to be armed when committing burglary. Racial differences were strongest in prison behavior. In Texas, blacks had a much higher rate of infractions; in California, whites did.

CONCLUSIONS

Before discussing our conclusions, we emphasize again that, whenever the data were sufficient, our analyses of system decisions and criminal behavior controlled for the most obvious variables that could reasonably account for apparent racial differences. In these comparisons, then, our offenders are "interchangeable" except for race. It is also well to remember that our data came from only three states. Moreover, because our self-report data came from prisoners, conclusions drawn from those data are not necessarily applicable to the criminal population at large.

Explaining Disparities in Case Processing and Time Served

At most major decision points, the criminal justice system does not discriminate against minorities, but race does affect prefiling release, sentence type and length imposed, and length of sentence served.

As Sec. IV indicated, minorities are clearly overrepresented in the arrest population, relative to their percentage of the general population. However, analysis of the RIS data shows that they are not overrepresented in the arrest population, relative to the number of crimes they actually commit. Nor do they have a higher probability than whites of being arrested for those crimes.

Despite these findings, the OBTS analysis raises a question that the study could not answer: If blacks and Hispanics are not being overarrested, why are police and prosecutors so much more likely to let them go without filing charges? One possibility is that the police more often arrest minorities on "probable-cause" evidence that subsequently fails to meet the filing standard of "evidence beyond a reasonable doubt." Assuming that the police arrest all races on similar evidence, why should that evidence fail to hold in minority cases?

Prior research may throw some light on this phenomenon. As Sec. IV showed, the vast majority of crimes committed do not result in arrest. For most types of crime, the probability of arrest is less than 15 percent. Research has shown that arrests depend heavily on witnesses or victims identifying or carefully describing the suspect (Greenwood, Chaiken, and Petersilia, 1977). The data show that prosecutors have a more difficult time making cases against minorities "beyond a reasonable doubt" because of problems with victim and witness identifications. Research has shown that both white and black witnesses and victims have a harder time making positive identifications of minority suspects than of white suspects.[1] Moreover, studies have shown that crimes against minority victims are most often committed by minority offenders, very often acquaintances. After the arrest, victims frequently refuse to prosecute, withdraw the identification, or refuse to testify.

Such "evidentiary" problems would help explain the disproportionate release rates for minorities, and the study found another racial difference in case processing that may account for more of this disproportion. The OBTS data show that more white than minority suspects were arrested with a warrant in the study period. Because the criteria for issuing a warrant are essentially the same as those for filing criminal charges, cases involving warrants would be less likely to develop evidentiary problems after arrest.

Although the use of warrants may explain why more minority than white suspects are released after arrest, it raises a provocative question: Why are the police apparently more hesitant to arrest white than minority suspects without a warrant? Again, it may be that it is harder to make a case worth filing against minority suspects. Yet, by taking the trouble to get warrants to arrest whites, the police implicitly indicate that the reverse is true. Or, their actions may reveal that they think it is "riskier" to arrest whites on "probable cause." They may assume that minorities are less likely than white suspects to make false arrest charges or other kinds of trouble if a case is not filed. Whatever their reasons, the racial differences in warrant arrests and release rates suggest that the police operate on different assumptions when arresting minorities and whites.

Other findings of the study tend to reinforce the hypothesis that the system implicitly regards minorities differently from white offenders. Controlling for seriousness of offense, for prior record, for prison violence—in short, the most important factors that are said to influence sentencing and parole decisions—the analysis still found that blacks and Hispanics are less likely to be given probation, more likely to receive *prison* sentences, more likely to get longer sentences, and more likely to serve a longer time in prison.

---

[1]Frequently, witnesses or victims who were supportive at the arrest stage become less cooperative as the case proceeds. In fact, one of the most important factors affecting case mortality is the victim's desire to want the criminal proceedings disbanded altogether (Gottfredson and Gottfredson, 1982). This is a common occurrence when there is a prior relationship between the victim and the defendant (Vera Institute of Justice, 1977). It also occurs when the victim has been intimidated or feels threatened by the defendant or by aspects of the criminal justice system. Research has also shown that a major factor distinguishing cooperative from uncooperative victims is simple confusion about where they were supposed to appear or what they were supposed to do when they got there (Hamilton, 1979). It is conceivable that these aspects might be more prevalent in cases involving minority defendants.

As Fig. 1.2 has shown, in very serious crimes—where there is less room for discretion in sentencing—blacks are represented about equally in the arrest and prison populations. In other words, the prevalence of these crimes among blacks primarily dictates their numbers in the prison population. However, as we move to property crimes, the disparity between the black proportion of the arrest population and the prison population becomes quite wide. This disparity implies that probation officers, judges, and parole boards are exercising discretion in sentencing and/or release decisions. In making these decisions, they are evidently responding to offenders in ways that result in *de facto* discrimination against blacks. The same is true for Hispanics, who *served* even longer time than blacks.

It is possible that the racial differences in the length and type of sentence imposed reflect in part the racial differences in plea bargaining and jury trials noted in Sec. III. Fully 92 percent of white defendants were convicted by plea bargaining, compared with 85 percent for black and 87 percent for Hispanic defendants. Those numbers imply the total percentages that engaged in plea bargaining—since, by nature, plea bargaining virtually ensures conviction. However, it also virtually guarantees a reduced charge and/or lighter sentencing. When defendants who do not plea bargain go to trial, they generally receive harsher sentences. As one study recently concluded:

> The typical plea bargained case is much less likely to result in a state prison sentence, and is likely to receive a "much lighter" sentence at conviction than the typical case that goes to trial, and differences in sentencing between jury trials and plea bargained cases cannot be "explained away" by looking at the nature of the crime or the characteristics of the defendants in these cases (California Legislature, 1980, p. 59).

Our data show that of defendants prosecuted in Los Angeles County Superior Court, only 7 percent of whites were tried by jury, compared with 12 percent for blacks and 11 percent for Hispanics.

However, even if these mechanisms were found to account for some of the apparent racial differences in sentencing, the implication of racial bias simply shifts to another node in the system. Why should minorities plea bargain less and go to jury trial more than whites? If the differences represent defendants' attitudes and decisions, then the system is not actively responsible for this racial difference. However, it seems only just to try to find out why they make these decisions. If these differences reflect decisions by prosecutors or decisions by default, then the issue of bias returns. And it may reflect the kind of differences in the way minorities are regarded that are implied by the prefiling release rates for minorities.

The warrant and plea bargaining differences may indicate that white offenders simply know more about the system, and how to make it work for them, and that criminal justice officials are aware of this. However, in the case of plea bargaining, there may be other explanations. Other studies have shown that blacks are less able than whites to make bail and are more likely to have court appointed lawyers. Research has also shown that under those circumstances defendants are more likely to be convicted and to get harsher sentences. Apparently, both circumstances result in weaker cases for the defendant. In this situation, prosecutors may simply not be interested in plea bargaining. If the crime is serious enough and the prosecution's case strong enough, the prosecutor's office has little to gain by offering the defendant a lower charge or a reduced sentence in exchange for a guilty plea. It is also possible that unless a minority defendant is represented by a sophisticated attorney, the prosecutor will not regard him as a candidate for plea bargaining.

It may be that discrimination enters into sentencing in another way. Judges may hesitate to send white defendants to prison for two reasons. First, research indicates that in prisons where whites are the minority, they are rather systematically and seriously victimized by the dominant racial group. Intuition suggests a straightforward, if cynical, explanation for this behavior. Minorities see the "white world" as responsible for all the deprivation and brutalization they have suffered. In the closed world of the prison, where guards cannot see everywhere all the time, minorities may push the right of "majority rule" to its logical extreme: They victimize white inmates to retaliate against the white world outside. In most states, blacks now outnumber whites in the prison population. The racial differences in prison sentences may indicate judges' reluctance to send white defendants to black- or Hispanic-dominated facilities. Second, judges may regard whites as better candidates for rehabilitation, and therefore do not want to impose a prison sentence except as a last resort.

Research on sentence patterns lends support to the contention that the system "values" whites more than it does minorities. For example, Zimring, Eigen, and O'Malley (1976) found that black defendants who killed whites received life imprisonment or the death sentence more than twice as often as blacks who killed blacks. Other research has found this relationship for other crimes as well: Defendants receive harsher sentences if the victim is white and lesser sentences if he or she is black.[2] If harsher sentences do indicate that minority status equals lower status in the criminal justice system, that equation may

---

[2]Records show also that the higher the status (education, profession, wealth) of a victim, the harsher the sentence.

also help explain why minorities serve longer terms, all other things held equal, than white prisoners.

This hypothesis makes a distinction between discrimination against minorities and the status accorded blacks in the system that may be too fine to be useful. If such perceptions of status do account for racial differences in prefiling release rates, sentence severity, and time served, the effect is much the same as it would be with overt and explicit racial bias—and probably harder to reform. Considering that the criminal justice system is supposed to represent "the people," it seems particularly unrealistic to expect it to accord higher status than society in general does to people who characteristically occupy the bottom rungs of the socioeconomic ladder. However, the issue of socioeconomic characteristics provides another way of explaining the racial differences revealed by the study.

Information Used in Sentencing and Parole

Different officials are responsible for cases at various points in the system, and may have dissimilar objectives. They use different kinds of information to promote these objectives. As the accused moves through the system, more information about him is attached to his folder and that information is weighted differentially. Police and prosecutors are primarily concerned with "just deserts." Their legal mission is to assure that criminals are convicted. They concentrate on information they need to make arrests and secure convictions—primarily information about the crime and about the offender's prior record—according to strict legal rules.

The court must decide whether conviction is warranted and pass sentence. Judges also consider the nature of the crime and prior record in weighing just deserts, but they also weigh the defendant's potential for rehabilitation or recidivism. The central question is whether returning him to society through probation or a lighter sentence will create a serious risk for society. In deciding on probation, jail, or prison and sentence length for an offender, they consider his conviction crime, prior record, *and* his personal and socioeconomic characteristics.

To provide the latter material, probation officers in most counties prepare a pre-sentence investigation report (PSR) that contains a sentence recommendation. It is significant that probation officers, who have a social mission, not a prosecutorial one, handle the screening for sentencing. Probation officers are more concerned with analyzing and understanding the person and his situation, and they tend to deemphasize the legal technicalities of guilt and convictability, leaving that job to the prosecutor.

In intent and methodology, the PSR has been described as an effort to determine the "social credit rating of the individual" (Wallace, 1965). Its scope is practically unlimited. It describes the subject's family background, marital status, education and employment history, past encounters with the law, gang affiliation, drug and alcohol use, and the like. Most important, the PSR is the key document in sentencing and parole decisions. Its recommendations are generally followed by the sentencing judge, and in many states its characterization of the defendant becomes the core of the parole board's case-summary file.

The influence of the PSR may help explain the racial differences in sentencing and time served: Minorities often appear in a bad light when they are assessed by such indicators of recidivism as family instability and unemployment. Blacks and Hispanics typically have more of the personal and socioeconomic characteristics associated with recidivism than white offenders have. When probation officers, judges, and parole boards use the PSR's objective indicators of recidivism as guides, they are often compelled to identify minorities as higher risks.

Our findings on time served suggest that these conjectures may be valid. Because of California's determinate sentencing policy, length of sentence imposed largely dictates length of time served. Thus, any racial disparities in time served there mostly reflect racial differences in sentencing. In contrast, Texas has a very individualized and highly discretionary parole process, which relies heavily on the kinds of information contained in the PSR. And there we find that parole decisions appreciably lengthen minority sentences—sentences that were longer at conviction to begin with.

Michigan provides the strongest evidence for our hypothesis. Since 1976, Michigan has based its parole considerations primarily on three indicators: length of juvenile record, violence of crime, and prison behavior. This practice seems to have overcome the racial disparity in length of time served. Although black defendants in Michigan receive sentences 7.2 months longer than those of whites (other factors held equal), they do not *serve* significantly longer sentences. We need to examine the relation of indicators used and time served in other states. However, the Michigan experience suggests strongly that when parole decisions are guided by such indicators, racial disparities in time served might be reduced.

While it seems ideally desirable to eliminate these disparities, some practical questions remain: By excluding socioeconomic and other extralegal indicators of recidivism, will parole boards be increasing the risk to society? Are those other indicators actually objective, race-neutral indicators of recidivism that should be used to keep potential recidivists off the streets, regardless of the racial disparities they cause in sentencing and parole decisions?

If these apparently objective indicators of recidivism are valid, the criminal justice system is not discriminating against minorities in these sentencing and parole decisions. It is simply reflecting the larger racial problems of society. If we believe this is so, the system cannot do much about it, and criminal justice research can do little more than suggest that racial differences in the system are unlikely to disappear until society solves its racial problems. However, other research and the RIS data suggest that the indicators of recidivism may themselves be less "race-neutral" than past research and practice have indicated.

Assessing the Indicators of Recidivism

The *overrepresentation* of minorities in aggregate arrest statistics has tended to obscure the fact that the criminal justice system and criminal justice research are, nevertheless, dealing with a criminal population that is half white and half minority. Unless minorities in that population have higher recidivism rates than whites, there is no reason why they should consistently be seen as presenting a higher risk of recidivism. There is clearly a much higher *prevalence* of crime among minorities, which largely accounts for their equal representation with whites in the criminal population. But there is no evidence that their recidivism rates are higher.

A minority male is almost four times more likely than a white male to have an index arrest in his lifetime: One in every two nonwhite males in large U.S. cities can expect to have at least one index arrest. However, the RIS data indicate that, once involved in crime, whites and minorities in the sample have virtually the same annual crime commission rates. This accords with Blumstein and Graddy's (1981) finding that the recidivism rate for index offenses is approximately .85 *for both whites and nonwhites.* Thus, the data suggest that large racial differences in aggregate arrest rates must be attributed primarily to differences in involvement, and not to different patterns among those who do participate. Under these circumstances, any empirically derived indicators of recidivism should target a roughly equal number of whites and minorities. In other words, even if recidivism among whites had different causes or correlates than recidivism among nonwhites, they should at least balance one another. They should not consistently identify nonwhites as more appropriate candidates for more severe treatment.

Then why does this happen? It may be due to the relative size and diversity of the base populations. For example, the black portion of the criminal population draws from not only a much smaller but also a more homogeneous population, socioeconomically and culturally. That is, these people are more likely than their white counterparts to have common socioeconomic and cultural characteristics. The white half of the criminal population comes from a vastly larger, more heterogeneous base. Individuals in it are motivated variously, and come from many different cultural, ethnic, and economic backgrounds. Consequently, the characteristics associated with "black criminality" are more consistent, more visible, more "countable," if you will, than those associated with white criminality. Moreover, because *prevalence* of crime is so much higher than incidence of crime (or recidivism) among minorities, characteristics associated with prevalence of crime among blacks (e.g., unemployment, family instability) may overwhelm indicators of prevalence for the entire criminal population. They may also mask indicators of recidivism that are common to both blacks and whites.

The findings on criminal motivation and economic need lend support to this hypothesis. Blacks rated economic distress much higher than "high times" and very much higher than "temper" as their motive for committing crime. They also rated it more highly than either whites or Hispanics did. Moreover, the black inmates were consistently identified as economically distressed by the study's criteria for economic need. These findings imply that socioeconomic characteristics are more consistently related to crime among blacks than they are among whites. Considering that blacks make up approximately half of the criminal population, their characteristics may have the same effect on indicators of prevalence and recidivism that the extremely high crime rates of a few individuals have on mean crime rates.

This is a real vicious circle: As long as the "black experience" conduces to crime, blacks will be identified as potential recidivists, will serve prison terms instead of jail terms, will serve longer time, and will thus be identified as more serious criminals.

IMPLICATIONS OF THE STUDY FOR RESEARCH AND POLICY

These findings and conclusions raise some compelling issues for criminal justice research and policy. The first priority for both will be examination of the indicators used in sentencing and parole decisions.

Questions for Future Research

Assessing the Indicators of Recidivism. The criminal justice system is moving toward greater use of prediction tables that measure an offender's risk of recidivism. These tables are based on the actuarially determined risk associated with such factors as prior record and employment. This "categoric risk" technique does not assume that the facts of each case are unique. Rather, it assumes that the risk of recidivism is distributed fairly uniformly among groups of individuals who share certain characteristics. Some experts contend that this more objective technique reduces racial disparities because it severely limits discretion and because the indicators are racially neutral. We have argued, however, that these indicators may only appear racially neutral; in practice they may substantially overlap with racial status.

We need to reexamine the statistical methods and the evidence used to develop these risk-prediction schemes. As we just mentioned in discussing the indicators, the minority half of the criminal population probably has more characteristics in common, especially socioeconomic characteristics, than the white half has. Consequently, these characteristics statistically overwhelm others that might more precisely indicate the risk of recidivism for both whites and blacks. Worse, using socioeconomic factors that correlate highly with race will have the same effect as using race itself as an indicator. That would undoubtedly be ethically inappropriate.

To isolate these indicators of recidivism, analysts will need a methodology that permits them to control for homogeneity in the minority (largely black) half of the criminal population. Researchers will then have to determine whether the resulting indicators still lead to more severe treatment of minorities. Assuming that we want a system that can discriminate between high and low probability of recidivism, we also need some standard of judicial review that balances the state's interest in accurate identification of recidivists against the imperative that group classifications should not be implicit race classifications.

For each indicator that has racial links, we need to ask: How much predictive efficiency would the state lose by omitting this indicator from its sentencing standards? Without it, could the state still adequately assess an offender's risk of recidivism? Thus framed, the issue is not whether prediction tables could (or should) be used, but to what extent the state should sacrifice a degree of predictive efficiency to promote racial equity. Obviously, characteristics showing personal culpability (for example, prior convictions) should always be seen as acceptable factors for assessing risk. Even if minorities have a disproportionate number of them, these characteristics indicate individual not group status.

Post-Arrest Release Rates and Evidentiary Problems. Research should be done on racial differences in post-arrest release rates. The RIS data show that the police are not simply overarresting minorities, relative to the crimes they commit, and then having to let them go. However, our findings do not discount the charge that the police arrest minorities on weaker evidence. Nevertheless, previous research suggests that the bulk of cases dismissed before filing involved uncooperative victims, and other research has suggested that minority cases more often have problems with victims and witnesses. Future research could help resolve these issues by asking why so many victims become uncooperative, whether the reasons differ in minority cases, and how often either the suspect or the criminal justice system itself intimidates victims or witnesses (Porter, 1982).

Racial Differences in Plea Bargaining and Sentence Severity. Racial differences in plea bargaining and jury trials might help explain why minorities receive harsher sentences. This study did not control for plea bargaining in analyzing racial differences in sentence severity. If future research establishes that plea bargaining does contribute to those differences, the next important research task would be to discover why minority defendants are less likely than whites to plea bargain and more likely to have jury trials. Do prosecutors consistently offer less attractive plea bargains to minority defendants, or do minority defendants simply insist more on jury trials?

Effect of Prisons' Racial Mix on Sentencing. This question deserves research attention: If judges become increasingly reluctant to send white offenders to prisons where blacks and Hispanics outnumber them, racial differences in sentence severity will widen, and racial disproportions in prisons will grow. It will not be easy to resolve this sensitive question empirically. The first task would be to establish that judges are indeed influenced by reports that white prisoners are commonly and seriously victimized where they are the minority race. The second task would be to establish whether these reports are valid. That will be even more difficult because prisons are closed societies where much that happens is never known, much less recorded, by administrators. If research did establish that those reports are valid, the criminal justice system would face harder issues than sentencing practices. Among the most serious might be pressure for segregated facilities.

How Prison-Gang Membership Affects Length of Sentence Served. We need to look at the influence of gang-related activities on length of sentence served and participation in prison treatment and work programs. We found that minorities serve longer terms in some states—even when we controlled for other factors. However, we did not have information on gang affiliation. In California, one out of every seven prisoners is currently held in administrative segregation, mostly for gang-related activities. Also, a greater proportion of the black and Hispanic inmates admit to gang membership. It may be that a greater proportion of minorities are in segregation because of gang affiliation, and that persons in segregation have restricted access to prison treatment and work programs. Since program participation affects release decisions—either in earning good-time credits or gaining parole release—gang affiliation may be an important contributing factor to racial differences in length of sentence served.

The Prison Environment's Influence on In-Prison Behavior. Some inmates who were predicted to be high infractors exhibited rather exemplary behavior. The question here is the extent to which their good behavior can be attributed to their physical surroundings, e.g., specific security measures, inmate-to-staff ratio, recreational facilities, the total size of their institution, the particular housing arrangements, and so forth.

The Connection Between Prison Violence and Idleness. Prison administrators face both rising violence and shrinking budgets. Research can help them cope by finding out more about the relationship between idleness and prison violence and by identifying the kinds of inmates whose participation in programs will reduce violence the most. It may be that participation in prison *treatment programs* significantly reduces infractions for *older* inmates, while *work assignments* have similar effects for *younger* inmates. Being totally "idle" may cause the most violence in inmates younger than 25. Empirically based models of the relationship between inmate characteristics, programs, and violence could help prison administrators allocate their resources to combat violence. These models are also needed as a long-range planning tool. Prison administrators need "baseline" data upon which to predict the effects that particular changes might have on the level of prison violence (e.g., changes in inmate characteristics, reductions in prison programming budgets).

Policy Recommendations

Definitive policy recommendations must await findings from some of these research tasks, but we can recommend some interim policy initiatives.

Police and prosecutors need to be more aware of the difficulty of getting adequate evidence with which to convict minority suspects. The high release rates for minorities suggest that minority suspects are not as likely as whites to be identified from lineups or elsewhere, and

that victims or key witnesses in minority cases often prove uncooperative after the arrest has taken place. Police and prosecutors may have
to take greater pains to secure trust and cooperation of minority victims and witnesses.

*The process of plea bargaining needs to be closely monitored for any
indications that the plea agreements offered minorities are less attractive than those offered to whites.* One means of assuring greater uniformity is to have a single deputy review all the plea negotiations.
Again, their unfamiliarity with and distrust of the system may cause
minorities to insist on a trial. If so, they should be informed that
sentences resulting from jury trials are generally more severe.

*Judges and probation officers must begin to distinguish between in-
formation concerning the defendant's personal culpability and information that reflects his social status.* The latter information may not
be as racially neutral or objective as previous research has indicated.
Until the indicators of recidivism presently used have been reanalyzed, we recommend that officials weight the criminal's characteristics more heavily than socioeconomic indicators in sentencing and
parole decisions—but not so heavily that they ignore clear indications
that the defendant presents a risk to society.

*To reduce prison violence, prison administrators should allocate
available programs, particularly prison jobs, to young inmates.* We
know that younger inmates are responsible for most prison violence
and that the level of violence can be reduced by having inmates participate in work and treatment programs.

Finally, rehabilitation should be given another look. It is perhaps
unfashionable to speak of rehabilitation when prison administrators
are faced with shrinking budgets, increased population, and more
troublesome inmates. Most administrators have been forced to assign
low priorities to treatment programs. Although rehabilitation programs have not yet fulfilled their initial promise, this trend's long-
range implications are troubling. How can we hope to reduce an offender's propensity for crime if his ability to secure employment or
abstain from daily drug and alcohol use has not changed or has grown
weaker since he was imprisoned?

The RIS data show that most inmates do not receive the treatment
that they need. Two-thirds of the inmates who were chronically unemployed preceding their imprisonment failed to participate in vocational training programs. Two-thirds of those with alcohol problems did
not receive alcohol treatment. And perhaps the biggest and most disturbing gap is in drug treatment. Approximately 20 to 40 percent of
the inmates were very active drug users by their own admission and
by official classifications, and they related drug use to their criminal
activities. But in both California and Texas, 95 percent of inmates

who needed drug treatment failed to get it. (In Michigan, about half of the drug-dependent inmates received treatment.) For most programs, inmates who needed treatment reported that they failed to participate because they "did not have time" or believed they did not need the program. However, about one-third reported that they did not participate in drug programs because there were no programs. This is especially disturbing in light of the fact that over half of those who did participate in drug programs believed that the program had benefited them in a number of ways, including an expected reduction in future criminality.

Our data show further that advances in treating the drug-dependent offender could significantly reduce crime. The RIS data on inmates show that the extent of drug use is one of the strongest predictors of a person's involvement in serious and frequent crime (Chaiken and Chaiken, 1982). Given this evidence, it seems imperative that prison administrators resist the current trend of cutting rehabilitation programs in general, and drug treatment programs specifically, in order to stretch the funds they have available. Such "economy" may prove very expensive in the end.

Like other public institutions, the criminal justice system faces tightening economic restrictions. It has had to make hard choices among policies, programs, and research priorities. However, we believe that there could be no more important priority for policy and research than attempting to identify those aspects of the system that permit harsher treatment of minorities.

This study leaves us with guarded optimism concerning the system and the personnel who operate it. We did not find widespread, conscious prejudice against certain racial groups. Rather, when we found racial disparities, they seem to have developed because the system adopted procedures without analyzing their possible effects on different racial groups. Criminal justice research and policy now need to look behind the scenes. They need to focus on the key actors and their decisionmaking: what information they use, how accurate it is, and whether its imposition affects particular racial groups unfairly.

Appendix A

OBTS REGRESSION ANALYSIS OF
PRISON/NOT PRISON

(If convicted of robbery in L.A. Superior Court in 1980)

Name	Description	Parameter Estimate	Standard Error	T-Ratio	Prob > |T|
INTERCEPT		0.40	0.01	20.9	0.00
UNDER20	Age < 20	-0.19	0.01	-11.6	0.00
AGE2022	Age 20-22	-0.02	0.01	-1.8	0.06
OVER2328	Age 23-28	0.10	0.01	6.2	0.00
OVER28	Age 29+	0.12	0.02	5.9	0.00
ROBHOM	Convicted of Rob or Hom	0.22	0.01	13.9	0.00
ASSAULT	Convicted of Assault	-0.01	0.02	-0.7	0.45
BURGTHFT	Convicted of Burg or Theft	-0.06	0.02	-3.1	0.00
MISCRM	Convicted of Misc Crime	-0.13	0.02	-4.6	0.00
NCOMTMNT	Criminal Status None	-0.09	0.01	-6.3	0.00
PAROLE	Criminal Status Parole	0.10	0.02	5.2	0.00
PROBATN	Criminal Status Probation	-0.01	0.01	-1.0	0.31
NOPRIOR	No Prior Record	-0.17	0.02	-6.5	0.00
MISCPRIR	Prior Jail or Less	-0.05	0.01	-2.9	0.00
ONEPRIS	One Prior Prison	0.10	0.02	3.8	0.00
TWOPRIS	2+ Prior Prison	0.12	0.03	3.3	0.00
WHITE	Race-White	-0.01	0.01	-0.8	0.37
BLACK	Race-Black	0.02	0.01	2.2	0.02
HISPANIC	Race-Hispanic	-0.01	0.01	-1.0	0.28

SSE	383.59	F RATIO	53.71
DFE	2082	PROB>F	0.0001
MSE	0.18	R-SQUARE	0.2511

Appendix B

RIS REGRESSION ANALYSIS ON LENGTH OF COURT-IMPOSED MINIMUM SENTENCE

CALIFORNIA
DESCRIPTIVE STATISTICS

Name	Mean	Standard Deviation
INTERCEPT	1.000	0.000
SENSELF	38.397	18.542
LNSENLEN	3.532	0.491
SENMIN	33.291	17.394
LNSENMIN	3.362	0.555
SENMAX	46.996	22.211
LNSENMAX	3.724	0.528
AGE2	0.357	0.480
AGE3	0.321	0.467
AGE4	0.168	0.375
HOMICIDE	0.102	0.304
PERSONAL	0.198	0.399
ROBBERY	0.354	0.479
JUVPRIOR	0.033	0.179
JAILONLY	0.513	0.500
PRIORPRI	0.420	0.494
BLACK	0.364	0.482
SPANAMER	0.192	0.394
AGE1	0.152	0.359
PROPERTY	0.344	0.475
NOPRIOR	0.033	0.179
WHITE	0.443	0.497

REGRESSION ON COURT-IMPOSED SENTENCE LENGTH

CALIFORNIA

		SSE	56689.74	F Ratio	15.99
		DFE	290	Prob>F	0.0001
DEP VAR:SENMIN		MSE	195.481859	R-Square	0.3775

Variable	DF	Parameter Estimate	Standard Error	T Ratio	Prob>|T|	Variable Label
INTERCEPT	1	37.23	1.69	22.0	0.00	
AGE1	1	-3.88	1.87	-2.0	0.03	Less than 22
AGE2	1	0.56	1.32	0.4	0.67	22-26
AGE3	1	3.12	1.37	2.2	0.02	27-31
AGE4	1	0.19	1.73	0.1	0.91	Over 31
HOMICIDE	1	5.73	2.03	2.8	0.00	Convicted for homicide
PERSONAL	1	6.28	1.59	3.9	0.00	Convicted for serious personal crime
ROBBERY	1	4.05	1.34	3.0	0.00	Convicted for robbery
PROPERTY	1	-16.07	1.40	-11.4	0.00	Convicted for property crime
NOPRIOR	1	7.63	3.58	2.1	0.03	No prior record
JUVPRIOR	1	-4.40	3.77	-1.1	0.24	Juv. prior only
JAILONLY	1	-2.07	1.86	-1.1	0.26	Prior jail, no prior prison
PRIORPRI	1	-1.16	2.07	-0.5	0.57	At least one prior prison
WHITE	1	-2.62	1.12	-2.3	0.02	White
BLACK	1	-1.27	1.16	-1.0	0.27	Black
SPANAMER	1	3.90	1.37	2.8	0.00	Hispanic

DESCRIPTIVE STATISTICS
MICHIGAN

Name	Mean	Standard Deviation
INTERCEPT	1.000	0.000
SENSELF	51.085	30.370
LNSENLEN	3.749	0.629
SENMIN	48.904	31.856
LNSENMIN	3.621	0.789
SENMAX	79.079	23.730
LNSENMAX	4.298	0.443
SENMIN2	54.197	40.414
SENMAX2	96.372	36.551
AGE2	0.257	0.438
AGE3	0.226	0.418
AGE4	0.187	0.391
HOMICIDE	0.101	0.303
PERSONAL	0.315	0.465
ROBBERY	0.219	0.414
JUVPRIOR	0.012	0.112
JAILONLY	0.541	0.499
PRIORPRI	0.407	0.492
BLACK	0.665	0.472
AGE1	0.328	0.470
PROPERTY	0.363	0.481
NOPRIOR	0.038	0.192
WHITE	0.334	0.472

REGRESSION ON COURT-IMPOSED SENTENCE LENGTH
MICHIGAN

		SSE	242619.4	F Ratio	9.37
		DFE	303	Prob>F	0.0001
DEP VAR:SENMIN		MSE	800.724088	R-Square	0.2362

Variable	DF	Parameter Estimate	Standard Error	T Ratio	Prob>|T|	Variable Label
INTERCEPT	1	59.19	4.32	13.68	0.00	
AGE1	1	-8.60	2.82	-3.04	0.00	Less than 22
AGE2	1	0.06	2.77	0.02	0.98	22-26
AGE3	1	7.23	2.94	2.45	0.01	27-31
AGE4	1	1.29	3.22	0.40	0.68	Over 31
HOMICIDE	1	21.27	4.12	5.15	0.00	Convicted for homicide
PERSONAL	1	-5.68	2.74	-2.07	0.03	Convicted for serious personal crime
ROBBERY	1	3.86	3.06	1.25	0.20	Convicted for robbery
PROPERTY	1	-19.44	2.66	-7.29	0.00	Convicted for property crime
NOPRIOR	1	6.71	7.22	0.92	0.35	No prior record
JUVPRIOR	1	4.65	10.94	0.42	0.67	Juv. prior only
JAILONLY	1	-3.14	4.45	-0.70	0.48	Prior jail, no prior prison
PRIORPRI	1	-8.22	4.74	-1.73	0.08	At least one prior prison
WHITE	1	-3.64	1.70	-2.13	0.03	White
BLACK	1	3.64	1.70	2.13	0.03	Black

DESCRIPTIVE STATISTICS
TEXAS

Name	Mean	Standard Deviation
INTERCEPT	1.000	0.000
SENSELF	42.520	28.571
LNSENLEN	3.546	0.643
SENMIN	49.021	26.741
LNSENMIN	3.734	0.580
SENMAX	67.813	24.993
LNSENMAX	4.129	0.458
AGE2	0.350	0.477
AGE3	0.148	0.356
AGE4	0.178	0.383
HOMICIDE	0.065	0.248
PERSONAL	0.108	0.311
ROBBERY	0.205	0.404
JUVPRIOR	0.019	0.137
JAILONLY	0.577	0.494
PRIORPRI	0.354	0.478
BLACK	0.537	0.499
SPANAMER	0.108	0.311
AGE1	0.322	0.468
PROPERTY	0.319	0.485
NOPRIOR	0.048	0.215
WHITE	0.354	0.478

REGRESSION ON COURT-IMPOSED SENTENCE LENGTH
TEXAS

		SSE	268824.6	F Ratio	10.44
		DFE	459	Prob>F	0.0001
DEP VAR:SENMIN		MSE	585.674487	R-Square	0.2002

Variable	DF	Parameter Estimate	Standard Error	T Ratio	Prob>|T|	Variable Label
INTERCEPT	1	58.44	2.82	20.6	0.00	
AGE1	1	-6.93	2.04	-3.3	0.00	Less than 22
AGE2	1	-1.13	1.81	-0.6	0.53	22-26
AGE3	1	5.55	2.38	2.3	0.02	27-31
AGE4	1	2.51	2.40	1.0	0.29	Over 31
HOMICIDE	1	7.27	3.48	2.0	0.03	Convicted for homicide
PERSONAL	1	-2.77	2.87	-0.9	0.33	Convicted for serious personal crime
ROBBERY	1	8.40	2.37	3.5	0.00	Convicted for robbery
PROPERTY	1	-12.90	1.89	-6.8	0.00	Convicted for property crime
NOPRIOR	1	10.67	4.36	2.4	0.01	No prior record
JUVPRIOR	1	-7.39	6.31	-1.1	0.24	Juv. prior only
JAILONLY	1	-6.71	2.68	-2.4	0.01	Prior jail, no prior prison
PRIORPRI	1	3.43	3.05	1.1	0.26	At least one prior prison
WHITE	1	-1.95	1.77	-1.1	0.27	White
BLACK	1	1.85	1.65	1.1	0.26	Black
SPANAMER	1	0.10	2.41	0.0	0.96	Hispanic

Appendix C

RIS REGRESSION ANALYSIS ON LENGTH OF SENTENCE SERVED

VARIABLES IN REGRESSION MODEL, MEANS AND STANDARD DEVIATIONS

Name	Description	California (n=337)		Michigan (n=363)		Texas (n=583)	
		Mean	S.D.	Mean	S.D.	Mean	S.D
HOMICIDE	Most serious conviction homicide	.12	.32	.10	.30	.07	.25
PERSONAL	Most serious conviction against person (not robbery)	.19	.39	.31	.46	.11	.31
ROBBERY	Most serious conviction robbery	.35	.48	.22	.41	.20	.40
PROPERTY	Most serious conviction	.34	.47	.37	.48	.62	.49
AGE1	Less than 22 years	.15	.36	.33	.47	.33	.47
AGE2	Between 22 and 26 years	.36	.48	.26	.44	.32	.46
AGE3	Between 27 and 31 years	.32	.47	.22	.42	.15	.36
AGE4	Over 31 years	.18	.38	.19	.39	.21	.40
IDLE	No participation in treatment or work programs	.15	.35	.12	.32	.17	.37
TOTINF	Some infractions	.42	.49	.39	.46	.46	.50
SERINF	Some serious infractions	.24	.43	.30	.46	.24	.43
LTHS	Not a high school graduate	.50	.50	.60	49	.68	.47
PRIORPRI	Prior prison	.43	.50	.41	.49	.37	.48
STATEJUV	State juvenile prior	.38	.49	.26	.49	.16	.36
NOTMARD	Single	.47	.50	.62	.48	.52	.50
DAILYDRG	Daily drug use	.36	.48	.23	.42	.17	.37
WHITE	White	.44	.50	.34	.47	.37	.48
BLACK	Black	.37	.48	.66	.47	.52	.50
SPANAMER	Hispanic	.19	.39	--	--	.11	.31
NOTWORK	No steady jobs	.43	.50	.37	.48	.16	.37
PSYCHELP	Diagnosed as needing psychiatric help	--	--	.22	.42	--	--
RC22	Drinking problem	.30	.46	.29	.45	.27	.45
CUSTMAX	Maximum security	--	--	--	--	--	--

REGRESSION ON SENTENCE LENGTH SERVED
CALIFORNIA

SSE	94899.69	F Ratio	14.69
DFE	304	Prob>F	0.0001
MSE	312.170025	R-Square	0.3259

DEP VAR: SENSELF
    Respondents estimate of term

VARIABLE	DF	PARAMETER ESTIMATE	STANDARD ERROR	T RATIO	PROB>|T|
INTERCEPT	1	44.4	2.1	18.0	0.00
AGE1	1	-4.3	2.2	1.9	0.04
AGE2	1	-0.3	1.6	-0.2	0.83
AGE3	1	1.8	1.6	1.0	0.27
AGE4	1	2.8	2.0	1.4	0.16
HOMICIDE	1	12.5	2.3	5.4	0.00
PERSONAL	1	4.4	1.9	2.2	0.02
ROBBERY	1	1.3	1.6	0.8	0.40
PROPERTY	1	-18.3	1.6	-10.8	0.00
TOTINF	1	4.2	2.1	1.9	0.04
NOTMARD	1	-4.5	2.2	-1.9	0.04
WHITE	1	-2.4	1.3	-1.7	0.07
BLACK	1	-0.0	1.4	-0.0	0.96
SPANAMER	1	2.5	1.6	1.4	0.13
RESTRICTION	-1	0.0	0.0	0.4	0.62
RESTRICTION	-1	0.6	0.0	30.0	0.00
RESTRICTION	-1	1.3	0.0	46.9	0.00

REGRESSION ON SENTENCE LENGTH SERVED

MICHIGAN

	SSE	165284	F Ratio	26.06
	DFE	307	Prob>F	0.0001
	MSE	538.384240	R-Square	0.4331

DEP VAR: SENSELF
Respondents estimate of term

VARIABLE	*DF*	PARAMETER *ESTIMATE*	STANDARD *ERROR*	*T RATIO*	*PROB>|T|*
INTERCEPT	1	38.4	2.7	14.0	0.00
MONHOLE	1	2.8	2.7	1.0	0.29
AGE1	1	1.7	2.4	0.7	0.46
AGE2	1	-4.8	2.3	-2.0	0.03
AGE3	1	3.3	2.4	1.3	0.17
AGE4	1	-0.2	2.5	-0.0	0.92
HOMICIDE	1	24.2	3.3	7.2	0.00
PERSONAL	1	-5.4	2.2	-2.4	0.01
ROBBERY	1	-1.5	2.4	-0.6	0.53
PROPERTY	1	-17.1	2.1	-7.9	0.00
STATEJUV	1	5.2	3.0	1.7	0.08
CUSTMAX	1	27.5	3.0	8.9	0.00
RESTRICTION	1	-0.7	0.0	-10.3	0.00
RESTRICTION	1	3.0	0.0	43.1	0.00

REGRESSION ON SENTENCE LENGTH SERVED

TEXAS

SSE	390488.7	F Ratio	13.33
DFE	481	Prob>F	0.0001
MSE	811.826915	R-Square	0.2170

DEP VAR: SENSELF
Respondents estimate of term

VARIABLE	DF	PARAMETER ESTIMATE	STANDARD ERROR	T RATIO	PROB>|T|
INTERCEPT	1	48.0	2.4	19.6	0.00
MONHOLE	1	10.4	2.9	3.5	0.00
AGE1	1	-10.2	2.3	-4.3	0.00
AGE2	1	-7.8	2.1	-3.6	0.00
AGE3	1	4.7	2.7	1.7	0.08
AGE4	1	13.3	2.7	4.8	0.00
HOMICIDE	1	9.3	3.9	2.3	0.01
PERSONAL	1	-1.2	3.2	-0.3	0.69
ROBBERY	1	2.9	2.7	1.0	0.28
PROPERTY	1	-11.0	2.1	-5.1	0.00
PRIORPRI	1	8.8	3.1	2.8	0.00
WHITE	1	-5.3	2.0	-2.5	0.01
BLACK	1	2.4	1.9	1.2	0.20
HISPANIC	1	2.8	2.8	1.0	0.30
RESTRICTION	-1	0.1	0.0	3.5	0.00
RESTRICTION	-1	-0.3	0.0	-3.5	0.00
RESTRICTION	-1	-0.2	0.0	-3.5	0.00

Appendix D

RIS REGRESSION ANALYSIS OF PRISON VIOLENCE

DESCRIPTIVE STATISTICS

Variable	California (N=337)		Michigan (N=363)		Texas (N=583)	
	Mean	S.D.	Mean	S.D.	Mean	S.D.
Square root of the infraction rate[a]	.335	.353	.476	.421	.241	.341
Social						
Age[b]	11.006	4.807	10.153	5.474	12.077	5.212
Black	.356	.480	.683	.466	.530	.500
Hispanic	.196	.397	--	--	.103	.304
Criminal						
No. of prior prisons	.462	.754	.816	1.329	.746	1.308
No. of serious convictions	2.491	1.699	1.964	1.496	1.765	1.284
Crime type[c]	.558	.497	.504	.499	.322	.468
Age at first arrest	15.237	4.144	16.690	4.231	19.068	4.355
Juvenile record[d]	.483	.493	.547	.498	.233	.423
In prison						
Prison work[e]	.593	.477	.462	.477	.584	.476
Treatment rate[f]	.143	.153	.205	.199	.176	.218
Months in prison	16.691	11.821	21.749	20.702	16.902	17.031
Missing prison work[g]	--	--	.088	.284	--	--

[a]Square root of weighted infraction score divided by months in prison.

[b]We subtracted 16 from all inmate ages to reduce their magnitude.

[c]Nonviolent offense--0, violent offense--1.

[d]Minor juvenile record--0, major juvenile record--1.

[e]No prison work--0, prison work--1.

[f]Number of treatment programs participated in, divided by months in prison.

[g]Not missing information--0, missing information--1.

RESULTS OF REGRESSION ANALYSES ON THE SQUARE ROOT
OF WEIGHTED INFRACTION RATES, BY STATE

Variable	California (N=337)		Michigan (N=363)		Texas (N=583)	
	T-Ratio	Prob>:T:	T-Ratio	Prob>:T:	T-Ratio	Prob>:T:
Constant	.803	7.230*	.999	7.647*	.800*	11.896
Social						
Age	-.023	-4.608*	-.039	-8.179*	-.033	-10.359*
Black	-.108	-2.686*	.063	1.531	.077	3.007*
Hispanic	-.017	- .339	--	--	.049	1.185
Criminal						
No. of prior prisons	.006	.161	-.016	-.819	.022	1.503
No. of serious convictions	-.009	-.750	-.019	-1.244	-.020	-1.689**
Crime type	.039	.995	-.125	-3.227*	.002	.007
Age at first arrest	-.007	-1.423	-.005	-.798	-.001	-.342
Juvenile record	.019	.432	-.007	-1.154	-.007	-.245
In prison						
Prison work	-.073	-1.935**	-.056	-1.449	-.175	-6.904
Treatment rate	-.332	-2.682*	-.070	-.691	-.250	-4.322*
Months in prison	-.001	- .491	.002	1.575	.001	1.162
Missing prison work	--	--	.127	1.939**	--	--
Estimated standard deviation of regression	.353		.421		.341	
R^2	.189		.347		.348	
F	6.279*		15.524*		25.378*	
Degrees of freedom	(12,324)		(12,350)		(12,570)	

*Significant at the .01 level.
**Significant at the .10 level.

REFERENCES

Arnold, William R., "Race and Ethnicity Relative to Other Factors in Juvenile Court Dispositions," *American Journal of Sociology,* Vol. 77, 1971.

Atkins, Burton, and Mark Pogrebin (eds.), *The Invisible Justice System: Discretion and the Law,* Anderson Publishing Co., Cincinnati, Ohio, 1978.

Bailey, D'Army, "Inequities of the Parole System in California," *Howard Law Journal,* Vol. 17, 1973.

Baker, Timothy, Fredrica Mann, and C. Jack Friedman, "Selectivity in the Criminal Justice System," *Prison Journal,* Vol. 55, No. 1, 1975.

Bennett, Lawrence, "The Study of Violence in California Prisons: A Review with Policy Implications," in Albert K. Cohen (ed.), *Prison Violence,* D.C. Heath and Company, Lexington, Massachusetts, 1976.

Bernstein, Ilene N., W. R. Kelly, and P. A. Doyle, "Societal Reaction to Deviants: The Case of Criminal Defendants," *American Sociological Review,* Vol. 42, 1977.

Black, Donald J., "The Production of Crime Rates," *American Sociological Review,* Vol. 35, 1970.

Black, Donald J., and Albert J. Reiss, Jr., "Police Control of Juveniles," *American Sociological Review,* Vol. 35, 1970.

Blumstein, Alfred, "On the Racial Disproportionality of United States Prison Populations," *The Journal of Criminal Law and Criminology,* Vol. 73, No. 3, 1982.

Blumstein, Alfred, and Jacqueline Cohen, "Estimation of Individual Crime Rates from Arrest Records," *Journal of Criminal Law and Criminology,* Vol. 70, No. 4, 1979.

Blumstein, Alfred, and Elizabeth Graddy, "Prevalence and Recidivism in Index Arrests: A Feedback Model Approach," *Law and Society Review,* Vol. 16, No. 2, 1982.

Bolte, Gordon, "Institutional Disobedience in a Maximum-Security Prison," *Offender Rehabilitation,* Vol. 3, Fall 1978.

Brewer, David, "Race and Prison Terms," unpublished manuscript, California Youth Authority, Sacramento, 1979.

Brown, Barry, and John Spevacek, *Disciplinary Offenses and Disciplinary Offenders Under Two Correctional Climates,* District of

Columbia Department of Corrections, Research Report No. 17, September 1969.

Bullock, Henry Allen, "Significance of the Racial Factor in the Length of Prison Sentences," *Journal of Criminal Law, Criminology, and Police Science,* Vol. 52, 1961.

Burke, Peter J., and Austin T. Turk, "Factors Affecting Postarrest Dispositions: A Model for Analysis," *Social Problems,* Vol. 2, 1975.

California Department of Justice, *Adult Felony Arrest Dispositions in California,* Bureau of Criminal Statistics and Special Services, Sacramento, California, 1981.

——, *Crime and Delinquency in California,* Bureau of Criminal Statistics and Special Services, Sacramento, California, 1978, 1979.

California State Legislature, *Plea Bargaining,* Sacramento, California, 1980.

Carroll, Leo, and Margaret E. Mondrick, "Racial Bias in the Decision to Grant Parole," *Law and Society Review,* Vol. 11, No. 1, Fall 1976, pp. 93-107.

Carter, Robert, "The Presentence Report and the Decisionmaking Process," *Journal of Research in Crime and Delinquency,* Vol. 4, 1967.

——, *The Presentence Investigation Handbook,* U.S. Department of Justice, Washington, D.C., 1978.

Chaiken, Jan, and Marcia Chaiken, *Varieties of Criminal Behavior,* The Rand Corporation, R-2814-NIJ, 1982.

Chaiken, Jan M., John E. Rolph, and Robert L. Houchens, *Methods for Estimating Crime Rates of Individuals,* The Rand Corporation, R-2730-NIJ, March 1981.

Chambliss, W. J., and R. H. Nagasawa, "On the Validity of Official Statistics: A Comparative Study of White, Black, and Japanese High School Boys," *Journal of Research in Crime and Delinquency,* Vol. 6, 1969.

Chiricos, Theodore B., and Gordon P. Waldo, "Socioeconomic Status and Criminal Sentencing: An Empirical Assessment of a Conflict Proposition," *American Sociological Review,* Vol. 40, 1975.

Christianson, Scott, "Corrections Law Developments: Legal Implications of Racially Disproportionate Incarceration Rates," *Criminal Law Bulletin,* Vol. 16, No. 6, November-December 1980.

—— (ed.), *Index to Minorities and Criminal Justice,* The Center on Minorities and Criminal Justice, School of Criminal Justice, State University of New York at Albany, 1981.

——, "Racial Discrimination and Prison Confinement—A Follow-Up," *Criminal Law Bulletin,* Vol. 16, No. 1, 1980.

Christianson, Scott, and Richard Dehais, *The Black Incarceration Rate in the United States: A Nationwide Problem,* Office of

Criminal Justice Education and Training, U.S. Department of Justice, Washington, D.C., August 1980.

Clarke, Stevens H., et al., "Felony Prosecution and Sentencing in North Carolina," University of North Carolina at Chapel Hill, 1982.

Clarke, Stevens H., and Gary G. Koch, "The Influence of Income and Other Factors on Whether Criminal Defendants Go to Prison," *Law and Society Review,* Vol. 11, No. 1, Fall 1976.

Coe, Rodney, "Characteristics of Well Adjusted and Poorly Adjusted Inmates," *Journal of Criminal Law, Criminology and Police Science,* Vol. 52, No. 2, July-August 1961.

Coffee, John C., "The Future of Sentencing Reform: Emerging Legal Issues in the Individualization of Justice," *Michigan Law Review 1361,* Vol. 73, 1975.

Cohen, Lawrence, "Conferring the Delinquent Label: The Relative Importance of Social and Legal Factors in the Processing of Juvenile Offenders," Ph.D. Dissertation, University of Washington, Seattle, 1974.

Cohen, Lawrence E., and James R. Kluegel, "Determinants of Juvenile Court Dispositions: Ascriptive and Achieved Factors in Two Metropolitan Courts," *American Sociological Review,* Vol. 43, 1978.

Cohen, Lawrence E., James E. Kluegel, and Kenneth C. Land, "Social Inequality and Predatory Criminal Victimization: An Exposition and Test of a Formal Theory," *American Sociological Review,* Vol. 46, No. 5, October 1981.

Collins, James, *A Comparison of the Racial Distribution of Rape, Robbery, and Assault Offenders in Police and Victimization Data,* Research Triangle Institute, Triangle Park, North Carolina, 1977.

Collins, James, et al., *Criminality in a Drug Treatment Sample: Measurement Issues and Initial Findings,* Research Triangle Institute, Triangle Park, North Carolina, 1982.

Conklin, John E., *Robbery and the Criminal Justice System,* J.B. Lippincott Co., Philadelphia, New York, Toronto, 1972.

Cook, Philip J., "A Strategic Choice Analysis of Robbery," Chap. 10 in Wesley G. Skogan (ed.), *Sample Surveys of the Victims of Crime,* Ballinger Publishing Co., Cambridge, Massachusetts, 1976.

——, *The Role of Firearms in Violent Crimes: An Interpretive Review of the Literature, with Some New Findings and Suggestions for Future Research,* Duke University, Durham, North Carolina, May 1981.

Cook, Philip, and Daniel Nagin, *Does the Weapon Matter?* Institute for Law and Social Research, Washington, D.C., 1979.

Crosby, Faye, Stephanie Bromley, and Leonard Saxe, "Recent Unobtrusive Studies of Black and White Discrimination and Prejudice: A Literature Review," *Psychological Bulletin,* Vol. 87, No. 3, 1980.

Curtis, Lynn A., *Violence, Race, and Culture,* D.C. Heath and Co., Lexington, Massachusetts, 1975.

Dannefer, Dale, and Russell K. Schutt, "Race and Juvenile Justice Processing in Court and Police Agencies," *American Journal of Sociology,* Vol. 87, No. 5, 1982.

Dunbaugh, Frank M., "Racially Disproportionate Rates of Incarceration in the United States," *Prison Law Monitor,* Vol. 1, No. 9, March 1979.

Elion, Victor H., and Edwin I. Megargee, "Racial Identity, Length of Incarceration and Parole Decision Making," *Journal of Research in Crime and Delinquency,* July 1979.

Elliott, Delbert S., and Suzanne S. Ageton, "Reconciling Race and Class Differences in Self-Reported and Official Estimates of Delinquency," *American Sociological Review,* Vol. 45, No. 1, February 1980.

Ellis, D., et al., "Violence in Prisons: A Sociological Analysis," *American Journal of Sociology,* Vol. 80, No. 1, July 1974.

Feeley, Malcolm M., *The Process Is the Punishment,* Sage Publications, Beverly Hills, California, 1979.

Fehr, Larry, "The Disproportionate Representation of Racial Minorities in the Criminal Justice System of Washington State," Washington Council on Crime, Seattle, Washington, 1982.

Ferdinand, T. N., and E. G. Luchterhand, "Inner-City Youths, the Police, the Juvenile Court, and Justice," *Social Problems,* Vol. 17, 1970.

Flanagan, Timothy J., *Sentencing in Prison: The Relationship Between Conduct and Disposition in Prison Disciplinary Proceedings,* Criminal Justice Research Center, New York, 1980.

——, "Correlates of Institutional Misconduct Among State Prisoners," *Criminology,* Vol. 21, No. 1, 1983.

Foley, Linda A., *The Effect of Extra-Legal Factors on Jurors' Decisions,* University of North Florida, November 1980.

Forslund, Morris A., "Age, Occupation and Conviction Rates of White and Negro Males: A Case Study," *The Rocky Mountain Social Science Journal,* 1969.

Forst, B., J. Lucianovic, and S. Cox, *What Happens After Arrest,* Institute for Law and Social Research, Washington, D.C., August 1977.

Frazier, Charles E., E. Wilbur Bock, and John C. Henretta, "Pretrial Release and Bail Decisions," *Criminology,* Vol. 18, No. 2, August 1980.

Fuller, Dan, and Thomas Orsagh, "Violence and Victimization Within a State Prison System," *Criminal Justice Review*, Vol. 2, No. 2, Fall 1977.

Garber, Steven, Steven Klepper, and Daniel Nagin, *The Role of Extralegal Factors in Determining Criminal Case Disposition: Toward More Reliable Statistical Inference*, Carnegie-Mellon University, Pittsburgh, Pennsylvania, 1982.

Gibson, James L., "Race as a Determinant of Criminal Sentences: A Methodological Critique and a Case Study," *Law and Society Review*, Vol. 12, No. 3, Spring 1978.

Gold, M., and D. J. Reimer, "Changing Patterns of Delinquent Behavior Among Americans 13 Through 16 Years Old: 1967-72," *Crime and Delinquency Literature*, Vol. 7, 1975.

Gordon, Robert A., "Prevalence: The Rare Datum in Delinquency Measurement and its Implications for the Theory of Delinquency," Chap. 8 in Malcolm W. Klein (ed.), *The Juvenile Justice System*, Sage Publications, Beverly Hills, California, 1976.

Gottfredson, Michael, and Don Gottfredson, *Decisionmaking in Criminal Justice: Toward the Rational Exercise of Discretion*, Ballinger, New York, 1982.

Green, Edward, "Inter- and Intra-Racial Crime Relative to Sentencing," *Journal of Criminal Law, Criminology and Police Science*, Vol. 55, 1964.

——, "Race, Social Status, and Criminal Arrest," *American Sociological Review*, Vol. 35, June 1970.

Greenberg, David, "The Incapacitative Effect of Imprisonment: Some Estimates," *Law and Society Review*, Vol. 9, No. 4, 1975.

Greenfeld, Lawrence A., "Measuring the Application and Use of Punishment" (draft), National Institute of Justice, Washington, D.C., November 1981.

Greenwood, Peter W., "The Violent Offender in the Criminal Justice System," in Marvin E. Wolfgang and Neil Alan Weiner (eds.), *Criminal Violence*, Sage Publications, Beverly Hills, California, 1982.

Greenwood, Peter W., Jan M. Chaiken, and Joan Petersilia, *The Criminal Investigation Process*, D.C. Heath and Company, Lexington, Massachusetts, 1977.

Greenwood, Peter W., et al., *Prosecution of Adult Felony Defendants in Los Angeles County: A Policy Perspective*, National Institute of Law Enforcement and Criminal Justice, LEAA, U.S. Department of Justice, Washington, D.C., October 1973.

Hagan, John, "Extra-legal Attributes and Criminal Sentencing: An Assessment of Sociological Viewpoint," *Law and Society Review*, Vol. 8, 1974.

Hamilton, William A., "Highlights of PROMIS Research," in William F. McDonald (ed.), *The Prosecutor*, Sage Publications, Beverly Hills, California, 1979.

Hindelang, M. J., *Criminal Victimization in Eight American Cities*, Ballinger Publishing Co., Cambridge, Massachusetts, 1976.

——, "Race and Involvement in Common Law Personal Crimes," *American Sociological Review*, Vol. 43, 1978.

Hindelang, M. J., Travis Hirschi, and Joseph G. Weis, "Correlates of Delinquency: The Illusion of Discrepancy Between Self-Report and Official Measures," *American Sociological Review*, Vol. 44, 1979.

——, *Measuring Delinquency*, Sage Library of Social Research, Vol. 123, Sage Publications, Beverly Hills, California, 1981.

Hindelang, M. J., and M. Joan McDermott, *Juvenile Criminal Behavior: An Analysis of Rates and Victim Characteristics*, Analysis of National Crime Victimization Survey Data to Study Serious Delinquent Behavior, Research Monograph 2, National Institute for Juvenile Justice and Delinquency Prevention, U.S. Department of Justice, Washington, D.C., 1981.

Hirschi, Travis, *Causes of Delinquency*, University of California Press, Berkeley, 1969.

Hoffman, Peter B., and Sheldon Adelberg, "The Salient Factor Score: A Nontechnical Overview," *Federal Probation*, Vol. 44, Table IV, March 1980, pp. 44-52.

Hoffman, Peter B., and Lucille K. DeGostin, "Parole Decisionmaking: Structuring Discretion," *Federal Probation*, Vol. 38, December 1974.

Holland, T. R., and N. S. Johnson, "Offender Ethnicity and Presentence Decisionmaking," *Criminal Justice and Behavior*, Vol. 6, 1979.

Honig, Paul K., *The Prison Experience of Career Criminals: Current Practice and Future Considerations*, The Rand Corporation, P-6178, July 1978.

Inciardi, J., and C. Chambers, "Unreported Criminal Involvement of Narcotic Addicts," *Journal of Drug Issues*, Vol. 2, 1972.

Jacob, Herbert, and James Eisenstein, "Sentences and Other Sanctions in the Criminal Courts of Baltimore, Chicago, and Detroit," *Political Science Quarterly*, Vol. 90, No. 4, Winter 1975-76.

Jaman, Dorothy, *Behavior During the First Year in Prison, Report III—Background Characteristics as Predictors of Behavior and Misbehavior*, California Department of Corrections, Sacramento, California, March 1972.

Johnson, Elmer H., "Pilot Study: Age, Race and Recidivism as Factors in Prisoner Infractions," *Canadian Journal of Corrections,* Vol. 8, 1966.

Just, Bernice, "Bail and Pre-trial Detention in the District of Columbia: An Empirical Analysis," *Howard Law Journal,* Vol. 17, 1973.

Kalish, C., *Prisoners at Midyear 1981,* Bureau of Justice Statistics Bulletin, U.S. Department of Justice, Washington, D.C., September 1981.

Kleck, Gary, "Racial Discrimination in Criminal Sentencing: Critical Evaluation of the Evidence with Additional Evidence on the Death Penalty," *American Sociological Review,* Vol. 46, December 1981.

Klepper, Steven, Daniel Nagin, and Luke Tierney, *Discrimination in the Criminal Justice System: Critical Appraisal of the Literature and Suggestions for Future Research,* Carnegie-Mellon University, Pittsburgh, Pennsylvania, 1982.

La Free, Gary D., "The Effect of Sexual Stratification by Race on Official Reactions to Rape," *American Sociological Review,* Vol. 45, No. 5, October 1980a.

——, "Variables Affecting Guilty Pleas and Convictions in Rape Cases: Toward a Social Theory of Rape Processing," *Social Forces,* Vol. 58, No. 3, March 1980b.

Lizotte, Alan J., "Extra-Legal Factors in Chicago's Criminal Courts: Testing the Conflict Model of Criminal Justice," *Social Problems,* Vol. 25, No. 5, 1977.

Loftus, Elizabeth, *Eyewitness Testimony,* Harvard University Press, Boston, Massachusetts, 1979.

Marquis, Kent H., and Patricia Ebener, *Quality of Prisoner Self-Reports: Arrest and Conviction Response Errors,* The Rand Corporation, R-2637-DOJ, 1981.

McCarthy, John P., Jr., *Report of the Sentencing Guidelines Project on the Relationship Between Race and Sentencing,* Administrative Office of the Courts, State of New Jersey, 1979.

McCarthy, John, and Neil Sheflin, "Report on the Relationship Between Race and Sentencing," Administrative Office of the Courts, State of New Jersey, 1979.

McDonald, William F., Henry H. Rossman, and James A. Cramer, *Police-Prosecutor Relations in the United States,* Institute of Criminal Law and Procedure, University Law Center, Georgetown University, Washington, D.C., 1981.

Meyers, Martha A., "Predicting the Behavior of Law: A Test of Two Models," *Law and Society Review,* Vol. 14, 1980.

Monahan, John, Stanley L. Brodsky, and Saleem A. Shah, *Predicting Violent Behavior: An Assessment of Clinical Techniques,* Sage Publications, Beverly Hills, California, 1982.

Morris, Norval, and Michael Tonry (eds.), *Crime and Justice,* Vol. 2, The University of Chicago Press, Chicago, Illinois, 1980.

Myers, Louis, and Girard Levy, "Description and Prediction of the Intractable Inmate," *Journal of Research in Crime and Delinquency,* Vol. 15, No. 2, July 1978.

National Institute of Corrections, United States Department of Justice, "Minutes of Conference on Incarcerated Minorities," unpublished memorandum, 1979.

National Minority Advisory Council on Criminal Justice, *The Inequality of Justice: A Report on Crime and the Administration of Justice in the Minority Community,* Office of Justice Assistance, Research and Statistics, U.S. Department of Justice, Washington, D.C., September 1980.

Owens, Charles E., and Jimmy Bell (eds.), *Blacks and Criminal Justice,* D.C. Heath and Co., Lexington, Massachusetts, 1977.

Pannell, William C., *Sentencing Practices Under the Determinate Sentencing Law,* Board of Prison Terms, State of California, Sacramento, 1981.

Petersen, David M., and Paul C. Friday, "Early Release from Incarceration: Race as a Factor in the Use of Shock Probation," *The Journal of Criminal Law and Criminology,* Vol. 66, No. 1, 1975.

Petersilia, Joan, "Which Inmates Participate in Prison Treatment Programs," *Journal of Offender Counseling and Rehabilitation,* Vol. 4, No. 2, 1980.

——, "The Validity of Criminality Data Derived from Personal Interviews," in Charles F. Wellford (ed.), *Quantitative Studies in Criminology*, Sage Publications, Beverly Hills, California, 1978.

Petersilia, Joan, and Peter W. Greenwood, with Marvin Lavin, *Criminal Careers of Habitual Felons,* The Rand Corporation, R-2144-DOJ, August 1977.

Petersilia, Joan, Paul Honig, and C. A. Hubay, Jr., *The Prison Experience of Career Criminals,* The Rand Corporation, R-2511-DOJ, May 1980.

Peterson, Mark A., and Harriet B. Braiker, with Suzanne M. Polich, *Who Commits Crimes: A Survey of Prison Inmates,* Oelgeschlager, Gunn & Hain Publishers, Inc., Cambridge, Massachusetts, 1981.

Peterson, Mark, et al., *Survey of Prison and Jail Inmates: Background and Method,* The Rand Corporation, N-1635-NIJ, 1982.

Piliavin, Irving, and Scott Briar, "Police Encounters with Juveniles," *American Journal of Sociology,* Vol. 70, September 1964.

Pope, Carl E., "The Influence of Social and Legal Factors on Sentence Dispositions: A Preliminary Analysis of Offender-Based Transaction Statistics," *Journal of Criminal Justice,* Vol. 4, 1976.

——, *Offender-Based Transaction Statistics: New Directions in Data Collection and Reporting,* National Criminal Justice Information and Statistics Service, LEAA, U.S. Department of Justice, Washington, D.C., 1975a.

——, "Postarrest Release Decisions: An Empirical Examination of Social and Legal Criteria," *Journal of Research in Crime and Delinquency,* Vol. 15, January 1978.

——, "Race and Crime Revisited," *Journal of Research in Crime and Delinquency,* Vol. 16, July 1979.

——, *Sentencing of California Felony Offenders,* National Criminal Justice Information and Statistics Service, LEAA, U.S. Department of Justice, Washington, D.C., 1975b.

Pope, Carl E., and William H. Feyerherm, "Race and Juvenile Court Dispositions: An Examination of Initial Screening Decisions," *Criminal Justice and Behavior,* Vol. 8, No. 3, September 1981.

Porter, Bruce, "California Prison Gangs," *Corrections Magazine,* Vol. 8, No. 6, December 1982.

Radelet, Michael L., "Racial Characteristics and the Imposition of the Death Penalty," *American Sociological Review,* Vol. 46, December 1981.

Reiss, Albert J., Jr., "Discretionary Justice in the United States," *International Journal of Criminology and Penology,* Vol. 2, 1974.

Rolph, John E., Jan M. Chaiken, and Robert L. Houchens, *Methods for Estimating Crime Rates of Individuals,* The Rand Corporation, R-2730-NIJ, March 1981.

Scott, Joseph E., "The Use of Discretion in Determining the Severity of Punishment for Incarcerated Offenders," *The Journal of Criminal Law and Criminology,* Vol. 65, No. 2, 1974.

Sellin, Thorsten, and Marvin E. Wolfgang, *The Measurement of Delinquency,* John Wiley & Sons, New York, 1964.

Shinnar, S., and R. Shinnar, "The Effects of the Criminal Justice System on the Control of Crime: A Quantitative Approach," *Law and Society Review,* Vol. 9, 1975.

Silberman, Charles E., *Criminal Violence, Criminal Justice,* Random House, New York, 1978.

Spohn, Cassia, John Gruhl, and Susan Welch, "The Effect of Race on Sentencing: A Re-Examination of an Unsettled Question," *Law and Society Review,* Vol. 16, No. 1, 1981-82.

Swigert, Victoria L., and Ronald A. Farrell, "Normal Homicides and the Law," *American Sociological Review,* Vol. 42, No. 1, February 1977.

Terry, Robert, "Discrimination in the Handling of Juvenile Offenders by Social-Control Agencies," *Journal of Research in Crime and Delinquency,* Vol. 4, 1967.

Thornberry, Terence P., "Race, Socioeconomic Status and Sentencing in the Juvenile Justice System," *The Journal of Criminal Law and Criminology,* Vol. 64, No. 1, 1973.

Tiffany, Lawrence P., Yakov Avichai, and Geoffrey W. Peters, "A Statistical Analysis of Sentencing in Federal Courts: Defendants Convicted After Trial, 1967-1968," *Journal of Legal Studies,* Vol. 4, No. 2, June 1975.

U.S. Department of Justice, "The Prevalence of Crime," *Bureau of Justice Statistics,* Vol. 4, Washington, D.C., 1982.

Unnever, James D., Charles E. Frazier, and John C. Henretta, "Race Differences in Criminal Sentencing," *The Sociological Quarterly 21,* Vol. 21, Spring 1980.

Vera Institute of Justice, *Felony Arrests: Their Prosecution and Disposition in New York City's Courts,* New York, New York, 1977; rev. ed., Longman, Inc., New York, 1981.

Wallace, John, *Aids in Sentencing,* 40 F.R.D., 433, at 433, 1965.

Williams, J. R., and M. Gold, "From Delinquent Behavior to Official Delinquency," *Social Problems,* Vol. 20, 1972.

Wolfgang, Marvin, "Quantitative Analysis of Adjustment to the Prison Community," *Journal of Criminal Law, Criminology and Police Science,* Vol. 51, 1961.

Wolfgang, M., R. M. Figlio, and T. Sellin, *Delinquency in a Birth Cohort,* University of Chicago Press, Chicago, 1972.

Wolfgang, Marvin E., and Paul E. Tracy, *The 1945 and 1958 Birth Cohorts: A Comparison of the Prevalence, Incidence, and Severity of Delinquent Behavior,* Harvard University and the John F. Kennedy School of Government, Cambridge, Massachusetts, 1982.

Wright, James D., and P. Rossi, *Weapons, Crime, and Violence in America,* U.S. Department of Justice, Washington, D.C., 1981.

Zalman, Marvin, et al., *Sentencing in Michigan,* State Court Administrative Office, Lansing, Michigan, 1979.

Zeisel, Hans, "The Disposition of Felony Arrests," *American Bar Foundation Research Journal,* No. 2, Spring 1981.

Zimring, Franklin E., Joel Eigen, and Sheila O'Malley, "Punishing Homicide in Philadelphia: Perspectives on the Death Penalty," *The University of Chicago Law Review,* Vol. 43, No. 2, Winter 1976.